OUR STORY

Union J

OUR STORY

with MARTIN ROACH

photography by ELISE DUMONTET

MICHAEL JOSEPH
an imprint of
PENGUIN BOOKS

MICHAEL JOSEPH

Published by the Penguin Group

Penguin Books Ltd, 80 Strand, London WC2R 0RL, England

Penguin Group (USA) Inc., 375 Hudson Street,
New York, New York 10014, USA

Penguin Group (Canada), 90 Eglinton Avenue
East, Suite 700, Toronto, Ontario, Canada M4P 2YR
(a division of Pearson Penguin Canada Inc.)

Penguin Ireland, 25 St Stephen's Green, Dublin 2, Ireland
(a division of Penguin Books Ltd)

Penguin Group (Australia), 707 Collins Street,
Melbourne, Victoria 3008, Australia
(a division of Pearson Australia Group Pty Ltd)

Penguin Books India Pvt Ltd, 11 Community Centre,
Panchsheel Park, New Delhi – 110 017, India

Penguin Group (NZ), 67 Apollo Drive,
Rosedale, Auckland 0632, New Zealand
(a division of Pearson New Zealand Ltd)

Penguin Books (South Africa) (Pty) Ltd, Block D,
Rosebank Office Park, 181 Jan Smuts Avenue,
Parktown North, Gauteng 2193, South Africa

Penguin Books Ltd, Registered Offices:
80 Strand, London WC2R 0RL, England

www.penguin.com

First published 2013

002

Copyright © Union J and Martin Roach, 2013

All photography by Elise Dumontet. Copyright © Elise
Dumontet 2013.

Additional photographs supplied by:
Paddy Balls, copyright © Paddy Balls, pages: *23, 27,
45, 52, 55, 72, 230–31, 232, 240–41, 242–3, 244–5, 246–7*
Rex, copyright © Rex, 2013: pages *73, 218*
Fremantle Media Enterprises, copyright © Fremantle Media
Enterprises, 2013, pages: *106–7, 112–13, 116, 118-19, 126–7,
144–45, 160, 162-3, 168–9, 170, 179, 182–3, 186,
188–9, 191, 194–5, 202–3, 206, 208–9*
Corbis, copyright © Corbis 2013, pages: *73, 120*

Every effort has been made to contact copyright holders.
The publishers will be glad to correct any errors or
omissions in future editions.

The moral right of the authors has been asserted

Set in Rockwell Std, Enamel, Trend Slab,
Trend Sans, Wood Bonnet

Colour reproduction by Tag: response
Printed and bound in Italy by Graphicom srl

A CIP catalogue record for this book is available
from the British Library

ISBN: 978-0-718-17866-6

CONTENTS

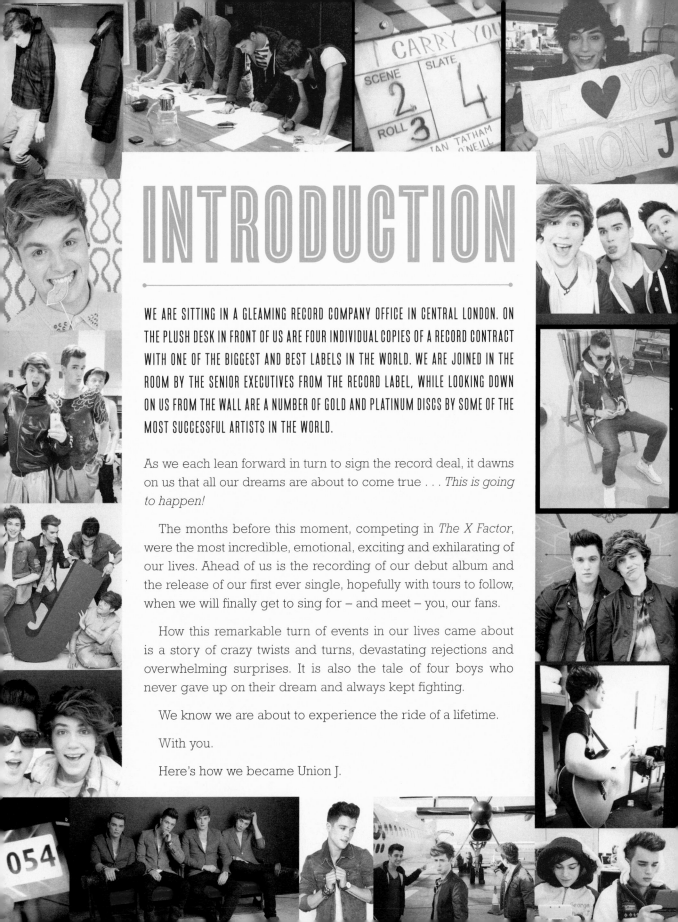

INTRODUCTION

WE ARE SITTING IN A GLEAMING RECORD COMPANY OFFICE IN CENTRAL LONDON. ON THE PLUSH DESK IN FRONT OF US ARE FOUR INDIVIDUAL COPIES OF A RECORD CONTRACT WITH ONE OF THE BIGGEST AND BEST LABELS IN THE WORLD. WE ARE JOINED IN THE ROOM BY THE SENIOR EXECUTIVES FROM THE RECORD LABEL, WHILE LOOKING DOWN ON US FROM THE WALL ARE A NUMBER OF GOLD AND PLATINUM DISCS BY SOME OF THE MOST SUCCESSFUL ARTISTS IN THE WORLD.

As we each lean forward in turn to sign the record deal, it dawns on us that all our dreams are about to come true . . . *This is going to happen!*

The months before this moment, competing in *The X Factor*, were the most incredible, emotional, exciting and exhilarating of our lives. Ahead of us is the recording of our debut album and the release of our first ever single, hopefully with tours to follow, when we will finally get to sing for – and meet – you, our fans.

How this remarkable turn of events in our lives came about is a story of crazy twists and turns, devastating rejections and overwhelming surprises. It is also the tale of four boys who never gave up on their dream and always kept fighting.

We know we are about to experience the ride of a lifetime.

With you.

Here's how we became Union J.

JJ HAMBLETT

1

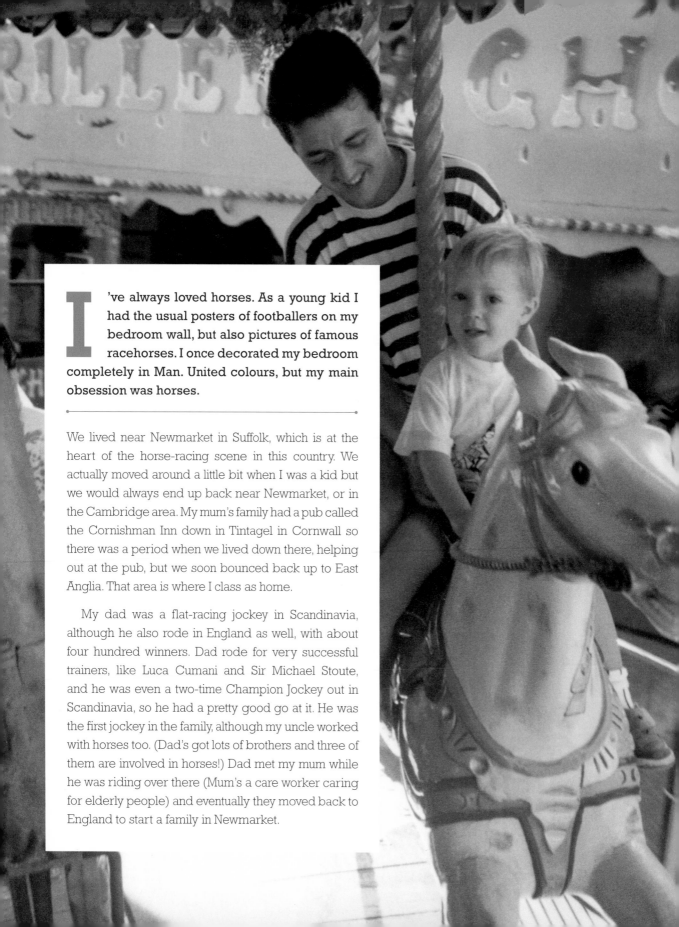

I've always loved horses. As a young kid I had the usual posters of footballers on my bedroom wall, but also pictures of famous racehorses. I once decorated my bedroom completely in Man. United colours, but my main obsession was horses.

We lived near Newmarket in Suffolk, which is at the heart of the horse-racing scene in this country. We actually moved around a little bit when I was a kid but we would always end up back near Newmarket, or in the Cambridge area. My mum's family had a pub called the Cornishman Inn down in Tintagel in Cornwall so there was a period when we lived down there, helping out at the pub, but we soon bounced back up to East Anglia. That area is where I class as home.

My dad was a flat-racing jockey in Scandinavia, although he also rode in England as well, with about four hundred winners. Dad rode for very successful trainers, like Luca Cumani and Sir Michael Stoute, and he was even a two-time Champion Jockey out in Scandinavia, so he had a pretty good go at it. He was the first jockey in the family, although my uncle worked with horses too. (Dad's got lots of brothers and three of them are involved in horses!) Dad met my mum while he was riding over there (Mum's a care worker caring for elderly people) and eventually they moved back to England to start a family in Newmarket.

'I'VE GOT ONE OLDER BROTHER, **ASHLEY**, AND ONE YOUNGER SISTER CALLED **OTEA** WHO ARRIVED WHEN I WAS SEVENTEEN, SO THAT'S QUITE A BIG GAP. I ACTUALLY USED TO SAY TO MUM THAT I'D LOVE A LITTLE SISTER BUT WE WERE ALL SURPRISED WHEN SHE ARRIVED. SO THAT WAS A FANTASTIC ADDITION TO OUR LITTLE FAMILY. LUCKILY MY SISTER'S COME OUT A LITTLE RASCAL; SHE'S A DIAMOND.'

I've got one older brother, Ashley, and one younger sister called Otea, who arrived when I was seventeen, so that's quite a big gap. I actually used to say to Mum that I'd love a little sister but we were all surprised when she arrived. So that was a fantastic addition to our little family. Luckily my sister's come out a little rascal; she's a diamond.

I am eighteen months younger than Ash and I've always looked up to him. We have always been really tight. In fact, when we were younger our closeness actually caused a bit of a problem, because we had our own language, we made our own words up. At first I guess the adults thought it was just a game but when it went on my mum panicked and took us to the doctor's. We also had a slight speech impediment and couldn't pronounce certain letters, so I guess my parents were right to be concerned. They analysed us and did some tests and decided that it was 'just a phase'. To be fair, though it lasted for some time it did eventually fade away. Fortunately, neither of us speak like that now!

Me and my brother always had a massively close connection; we did everything together. We loved the same things – horse racing, football – and we had ponies as kids and spent a lot of time together with them; it was brilliant. We had the odd argument, like brothers do, but I always looked up to him. I still do.

My childhood home was a bit like the Addams family! There's always mayhem in the Hamblett household! There was a lot of fun, loads of excitable shouting; it's just very loud, with kids running about and having a great time, and it's so nice to go back and have that normality. I love it, that's what I am used to, and with my little sister it's even more manic but great fun.

At school I was always a bit unpredictable because I liked some subjects, and I concentrated in those classes, but for other subjects I wouldn't try at all. Part of that slightly distracted demeanour I had about me was because all I ever wanted to do was race horses, to be a jockey. After school each day I would rush over to the ponies and spend time looking after and riding them – that was my life. Dad had stopped riding by then, but he still worked exercising horses for trainers and he had infected us with his love of horses, so both my brother and me were obsessed.

To be fair, I did love PE and Drama, although I didn't actually do Music at school. I wasn't especially academic – I felt I didn't need to be to become a jockey. I got very bored as well, to be honest. It seemed to depend on what day and mood I was in. Sometimes I'd be like, *Yeah, right. I will concentrate and get good grades*, but then the next day I would be less focused. Looking back, I wish I had made more effort at school.

My primary-school years were a lot of fun, though. My ultimate best mate at the time was Matt Low and we are still in constant touch. I always had loads of friends at school and we got up to the usual boys' games – you know, playing Manhunt and stuff like that. I used to hang around with this guy whose dad was a taxi driver and he'd generally be out all the time doing shifts, so after school loads of people would go round his house and sit there doing nothing. It was like the *Big Brother* house but full of kids!

'ACTUALLY, DESPITE WHAT YOU ARE NOW THINKING, I CAN'T TALK TO GIRLS THAT EASILY. EVEN NOW I AM QUITE SHY WITH GIRLS. REALLY WEIRD. I'VE ALWAYS BEEN A BIT INTIMIDATED BY THEM. IF I THOUGHT A GIRL WAS PRETTY, I'D GET REALLY NERVOUS AROUND HER AND NEVER KNOW WHAT TO SAY. I'M NOT ONE OF THESE PEOPLE WITH CHEESY CHAT-UP LINES.'

When I moved down to Cornwall I kissed a girl for the first time, I was in Year Four, very young! I remember kissing her in the chapel, proper romantic! We went and lit some candles and we were doing a prayer and stuff like that, and I kissed her. (I loved going down to Cornwall and still do; the pub is now owned by my Uncle Jeremy and his partner, Rochelle, and I love going down there to see Nan and just spend time and relax with them.)

When I was a lot older, we used to go to this club in Newmarket called De Niro's. It was a really big nightclub and there would be so-called 'Nappy Nights' for under-eighteens. Me and my friends would have competitions to see who could kiss the most girls. So I would probably call myself a lad, to be fair. Actually, despite what you are now thinking, I can't talk to girls that easily. Even now I am quite shy with girls. Really weird. I've always been a bit intimidated by them. If I thought a girl was pretty, I'd get really nervous around her and never know what to say. I'm not one of these people with cheesy chat-up lines. If I am out for a nice meal, I can chat all night, but I can never just go up to someone – can't do that. Fair play to people who can, but I find it awkward. I always try to be in relationships, genuinely.

Anyway, back to the story. I went to several different schools because we moved around a bit, but I generally had a good time. I didn't really find it unsettling and I made new friends easily. I was quite sporty, which always helps as a boy, so, for example, I was usually the fastest runner at school. I wasn't exactly Usain Bolt but I did used to win most races.

My time at school was enjoyable and I didn't get bad grades at GCSE; I enjoyed learning and I also enjoyed a few of the clubs and did a fair bit of drama at school too. A lot of my main school memories come from my time at Soham Village College, which was a wicked place to go. Like I said, though, as much as I enjoyed school, my head was usually full of riding; sometimes when I was at school, I'd work

hard in class then in the breaks I'd be watching the TV to see Channel 4 racing. Horses really were my life. There's a photo of me aged about two with me sat on one. So I was never scared of horses or ponies as I grew up. We would hire boxes at some stables somewhere and ride them out every day. My brother had a little pony called Greg, who was wicked, and I had a pony called Cameo, who was not so good! We'd bought her from the British Racing School and she was a lovely pony, but absolutely useless at jumping! We used to set up these show jumping competitions between ourselves and my brother always used to win on Greg. Cameo just wasn't a jumper, because all she was used to doing was going flat out. I'd never seen her fly over a jump: she used to canter up to them with me on her back, then suddenly stop dead still, dig her toes into the ground and send me flying off, and *only then* would she try to leap over it! She was a sweet little pony, but clueless.

Of course, people who have ponies as a kid don't necessarily go on to be jockeys; a lot of people have them just for the fun of it. But because of my dad's career, both me and my brother were really into the idea of becoming jockeys. That's why I ended up being a jockey.

I got my very first ex-racehorse when I was just thirteen, which is quite young really. The horse was called PG, short for Present Generation. He was what they call a hack, which is a horse used by trainers to help organise and look after the elite racehorses when they are out cantering and all that. So, for example, if someone falls off, the hack will go and bring the loose horse back.

However, the big moment for me came a year later when I sat on my first proper racehorse in training, which was a little filly called Fifth Addition. This was the real deal, so I was pretty scared! Before I cantered the horse I got so nervous. Dad was riding out with me and I was like, 'Dad, I can't . . . I'm too nervous, in case she gallops off with me.' Fortunately, she didn't and I was really proud of myself. I was like, *Yeah! I am a man!* I think my brother Ash was even younger when he rode his first racehorse. You get people in life who are born to ride, and you get people who have to work harder to do it. My brother was born to ride; I kinda wasn't! I had to work really hard and I still wasn't as good as him. He eventually went on to ride over eighty winners.

So you get the impression that racing was my thing! It was, but as I mentioned I was also massively into football and I really enjoyed singing too, increasingly so as I got older. We had a karaoke machine when I was a teenager and after school me and my mate would go to my house and sing all these covers. My family would go to karaoke nights at a local pub too and I'd do a few numbers, usually egged on by my mum. But I was very nervous being on stage; I'd stare at the words on the screen and not dare to turn round and see if anyone was looking at me. I used to absolutely poo myself. When I got past a certain age I used to need a drink in me just to get up there.

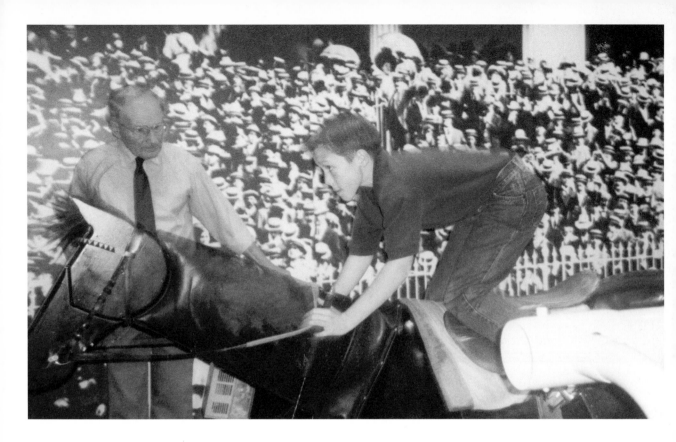

Back at secondary school, I actually started a band when I was fourteen called Cloud 9. I don't know why we called it that! There were three of us and we just sat there one day and said, 'Let's start a band!', which we did, but all that involved was us three saying we were in a band and thinking of a name. It never went any further than that. But I guess, officially at least, that was my first band. I think it lasted about a week!

At that time I was listening to a lot of boy bands. I'm not gonna lie, I've always been a sucker for Westlife. I love that kind of romantic music, great big ballads; they were massive for me. I've always listened to them. A lot of their songs, even when they do a cover, I still think they're amazing. They are a wicked band, and were a massive inspiration, especially for anyone who wants to be in a boy band. And the Backstreet Boys too sometimes. I remember crying over a girl for the first time; I'd been over to her house and then gone home and I was wondering if she liked me or not, so I rang her and I had Westlife's 'Miss You Nights' playing in the background! I was crying by this stage and I said, 'I was just wondering will you go out with me?' and she just went, 'Er, no!' I don't blame her! It's a little soppy looking back at it now!

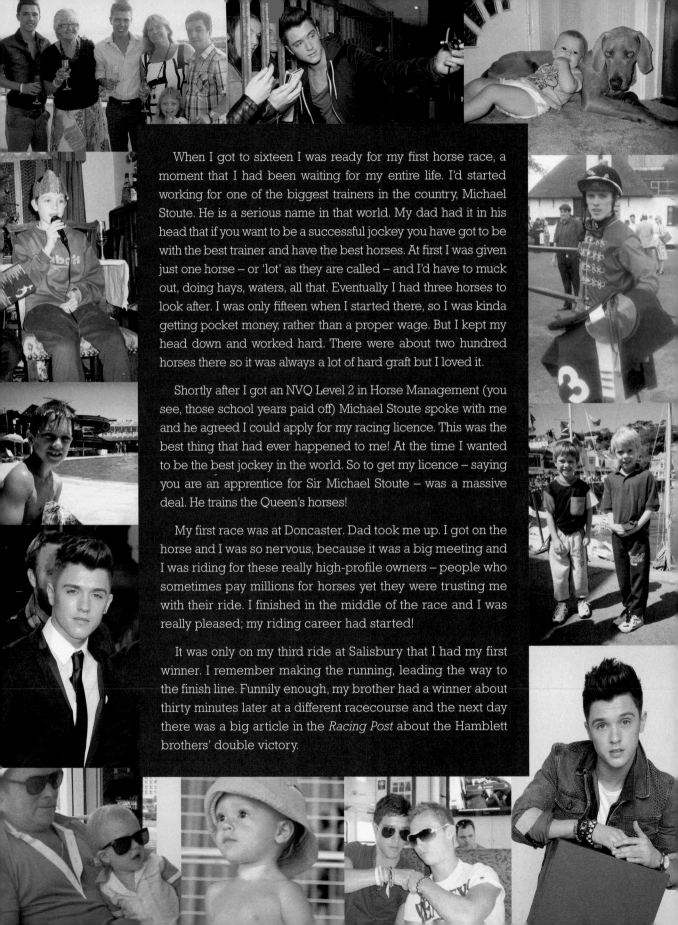

When I got to sixteen I was ready for my first horse race, a moment that I had been waiting for my entire life. I'd started working for one of the biggest trainers in the country, Michael Stoute. He is a serious name in that world. My dad had it in his head that if you want to be a successful jockey you have got to be with the best trainer and have the best horses. At first I was given just one horse – or 'lot' as they are called – and I'd have to muck out, doing hays, waters, all that. Eventually I had three horses to look after. I was only fifteen when I started there, so I was kinda getting pocket money, rather than a proper wage. But I kept my head down and worked hard. There were about two hundred horses there so it was always a lot of hard graft but I loved it.

Shortly after I got an NVQ Level 2 in Horse Management (you see, those school years paid off) Michael Stoute spoke with me and he agreed I could apply for my racing licence. This was the best thing that had ever happened to me! At the time I wanted to be the best jockey in the world. So to get my licence – saying you are an apprentice for Sir Michael Stoute – was a massive deal. He trains the Queen's horses!

My first race was at Doncaster. Dad took me up. I got on the horse and I was so nervous, because it was a big meeting and I was riding for these really high-profile owners – people who sometimes pay millions for horses yet they were trusting me with their ride. I finished in the middle of the race and I was really pleased; my riding career had started!

It was only on my third ride at Salisbury that I had my first winner. I remember making the running, leading the way to the finish line. Funnily enough, my brother had a winner about thirty minutes later at a different racecourse and the next day there was a big article in the *Racing Post* about the Hamblett brothers' double victory.

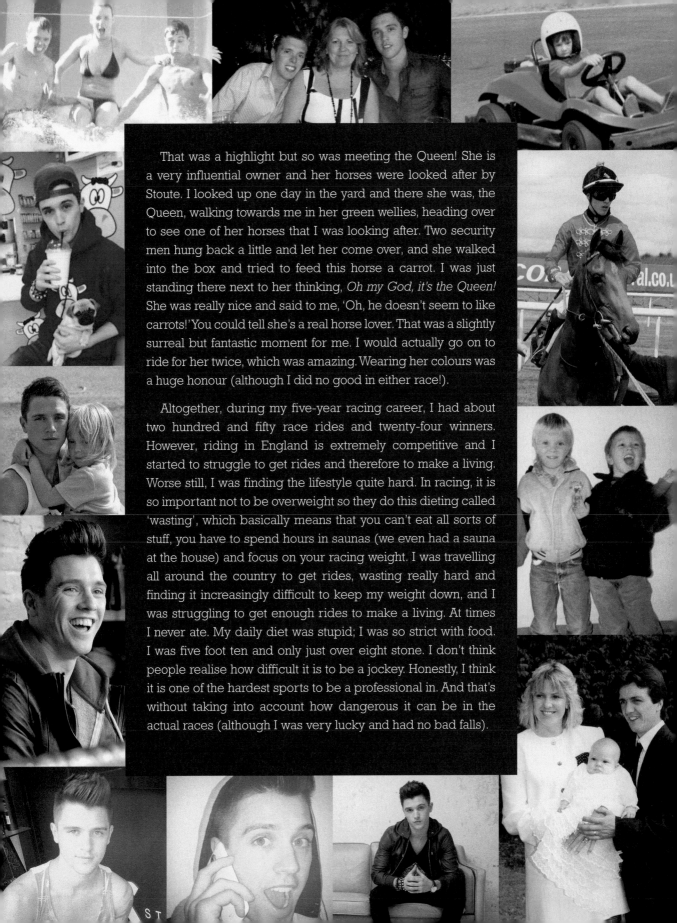

That was a highlight but so was meeting the Queen! She is a very influential owner and her horses were looked after by Stoute. I looked up one day in the yard and there she was, the Queen, walking towards me in her green wellies, heading over to see one of her horses that I was looking after. Two security men hung back a little and let her come over, and she walked into the box and tried to feed this horse a carrot. I was just standing there next to her thinking, *Oh my God, it's the Queen!* She was really nice and said to me, 'Oh, he doesn't seem to like carrots!' You could tell she's a real horse lover. That was a slightly surreal but fantastic moment for me. I would actually go on to ride for her twice, which was amazing. Wearing her colours was a huge honour (although I did no good in either race!).

Altogether, during my five-year racing career, I had about two hundred and fifty race rides and twenty-four winners. However, riding in England is extremely competitive and I started to struggle to get rides and therefore to make a living. Worse still, I was finding the lifestyle quite hard. In racing, it is so important not to be overweight so they do this dieting called 'wasting', which basically means that you can't eat all sorts of stuff, you have to spend hours in saunas (we even had a sauna at the house) and focus on your racing weight. I was travelling all around the country to get rides, wasting really hard and finding it increasingly difficult to keep my weight down, and I was struggling to get enough rides to make a living. At times I never ate. My daily diet was stupid; I was so strict with food. I was five foot ten and only just over eight stone. I don't think people realise how difficult it is to be a jockey. Honestly, I think it is one of the hardest sports to be a professional in. And that's without taking into account how dangerous it can be in the actual races (although I was very lucky and had no bad falls).

By this point, sometimes I would get a little nervous on a horse if he was tense, bucked or whipped, whereas when I was younger I would just laugh at that and sort it out. Racehorses are generally a lot more fried in the head than 'normal' horses – they have this racing brain and can be pretty nuts. It's not a job for the faint-hearted, so when I had a quiet horse to ride now I'd be chuffed. The trouble is that horses can read your nerves and that anxiety becomes a vicious circle.

So in 2009 I made the huge decision to hand in my licence. My racing career was over. I knew it was the right thing to do, but even so, after I had done it I was on a massive downer. My dream was over. I was only twenty-one. What was I going to do with the rest of my life?

So I did what many people do when they are uncertain about their life and their future: I went travelling. I say travelling, what I actually did was fly out to Australia with my then girlfriend to get away for the winter, get some sun and work in horse racing. I just wanted to feel more positive. But then, a couple of weeks before Christmas, we split up. We hadn't been getting on for a while but when we finally went our separate ways I was absolutely distraught. This girl was my first 'love', and, although we only went out for a year, I was still completely gutted. It took me months to get over her, I am not gonna lie.

'SO IN 2009 I MADE THE HUGE DECISION TO HAND IN MY LICENCE. MY RACING CAREER WAS OVER. I KNEW IT WAS THE RIGHT THING TO DO, BUT EVEN SO, AFTER I HAD DONE IT I WAS ON A MASSIVE DOWNER. MY DREAM WAS OVER. I WAS ONLY TWENTY-ONE. WHAT WAS I GOING TO DO WITH THE REST OF MY LIFE?'

So I was on the other side of the world, I'd just split up with my girlfriend, I'd already given up my dream of being a jockey, I had no money and I was scraping around, trying to get some cash. My head was everywhere, all over the place. I quickly ran out of work and on the day I got my last pay cheque I felt really miserable. What do I do now? I couldn't afford to fly home, and I remember Skyping my mum and crying my eyes out. Then I Skyped my brother and his lovely fiancée Flo came on and put me straight. She said I had to stay out there, that I would regret it if I didn't, and essentially she told me to 'Man up'!

I could just afford to pay for plane tickets to go to Sydney to try an alternative place to work, but it wasn't anywhere near as nice. So now I'd moved from a beautiful place in Melbourne to here, I still had no work and I only had twenty dollars in my pocket.

One day I bumped into this guy who I recognised from back home, Ben Morris, and it turned out he was from Newmarket so we got chatting. He'd also recently split up with his girlfriend so we hit it off immediately and now he's one of my best friends in the world! We had a good laugh and he lent me a few dollars to get me started and I gradually began to get back on my feet again. I got some work freelancing for different horse trainers and I was having a great laugh with Ben and various other people I'd made friends with. Now, looking back, the three months that followed were some of the best times of my life!

'WHAT DO I DO NOW? I COULDN'T AFFORD TO FLY HOME, AND I REMEMBER SKYPING MY MUM AND CRYING MY EYES OUT. THEN I SKYPED MY BROTHER AND HIS LOVELY FIANCÉE FLO CAME ON AND PUT ME STRAIGHT. SHE SAID I HAD TO STAY OUT THERE, THAT I WOULD REGRET IT IF I DIDN'T, AND ESSENTIALLY SHE TOLD ME TO **"MAN UP"**!'

*Chester Racecourse, one
of the places I raced.*

Everything happens for a reason and if I hadn't split up with my girlfriend and moved around Australia like I did, I wouldn't have met Ben.

Eventually it was time to return home and as soon as I did I got more work part-time, riding for horse trainers, including John Gosden; the people I worked with were fantastic, really special, but I still yearned to sing. I was still doing bits of karaoke and I was finding myself increasingly drawn to singing for a career. I'd be working away in the yard and always in the back of my mind I was thinking, *I'd love to be in a band . . .*

My optimism had returned by now so I excitedly put my name on to a website that showcases people who want to get into showbusiness and music. I also went for a couple of singing lessons with a local guy called David Hall who had been in *Phantom of the Opera* and he was wicked. I was aware there were thousands of lads trying to be singers but something told me I just had to give it a go.

I started applying for various auditions, which were almost always in London. I'd drive the two-hour trip down there, wait around and do the audition, come home and then either on the day or shortly after I'd get a 'No'. Then I got what seemed like a big break when I was offered a slot in a mixed band, which was really exciting, so I moved into a flat in London with them all for a month. There were seven of us, but like so many aspiring bands that soon fell apart and came to nothing.

I then got an audition for a band that was being put together by 19 Management, who most famously had looked after the Spice Girls, so this seemed like a really big chance, but although I got through the first round that was as far as I went. Another rejection. The nos just kept on coming and those trips up and down to London every few days began to feel longer and longer. I got a little bit of acting work, such as at a local theatre project where I was the lead man and also a short film about vampires that was apparently going to go to the Cannes Film Festival, but again, that never kicked off. I even tried modelling to get some money in but nothing was working. And all the time I was auditioning for bands constantly to no avail. I started to think, *This isn't going to happen.*

I was earning £270 a week exercising the horses but I wanted a house, my own place and a few nice things, and I couldn't do any of that on that kind of money. So I started looking in local papers for jobs. I went to this pub one day and a guy told me I'd be washing up dirty plates all day for three pounds an hour. I said no, and my spirits just kept getting lower.

I had always been very close to my grandad and nan. He had run this successful pub down in Cornwall and made a real mark in his life. He was a massive inspiration to me, because he was one of those people who'd started off with nothing and made something of himself at the end of it. He was a larger-than-life character; he didn't have a bad bone in his body and everybody knew him locally.

Then he got cancer.

It was a massive shock to the family. We thought Grandad would be there forever. He was always so healthy and fit – this big, strong man! But the illness wasn't going away and he was a shell of his former self. It was so upsetting. Then, God rest his soul, he passed away.

I was absolutely devastated. At his funeral I had to carry the coffin with my brother and four other people; we were at the front and I thought I'd be absolutely fine for Grandad, but then I walked in and his favourite Sinatra song, 'My Way', was playing and I just absolutely broke down. It was a proud moment for me and yet also the hardest of my life, carrying that coffin. It was horrible but I wanted to do it for him; I know he would have been proud of me doing it. I still think about him all the time. Growing up we used to have the best times with him and Nan in Cornwall and also go on amazing holidays to Turkey with them; they were two very special people in my life back then, and still are.

In an effort to lift the family's shattered spirits, Mum paid for us all to go to Turkey on holiday for her fiftieth birthday. We went, even Nan joined us thankfully, and we had a lovely break – real quality family time. I am a very family-oriented guy and I love spending as much time as possible with them. I still had nothing to come back to, though, and I was feeling battered, but while I was out there I got an email asking if I wanted to audition for a new boy band. I sent a clip back of me performing and the people organising the try-outs seemed keen, and then it was mentioned that one of the lads in the mix had auditioned for *X Factor* a few times, which really impressed and excited me. His name was Jaymi Hensley.

JAYMI HENSLEY

When I was a kid I thought I lived in the best house in the world. It was a three-bedroom house in Luton and I absolutely loved it. I had loads of friends nearby and as a kid I had the best time. When I was five my little cousin said to me, 'Your mum's having a baby and it's in her belly!' That was my brother, Aaron. I couldn't wait for him to be born and I was never threatened by this little new arrival; I loved him from the word go. I'd previously had my own bedroom but I thought it was the coolest thing in the world to be sharing a bedroom with my little brother. I remember vividly how when we were a bit older my dad did our room up; he spent an entire week completely kitting it out and we weren't allowed to peek. When he'd finally finished and we went in, he'd decorated it completely symmetrically, right down the middle, with my stuff on one side and Aaron's on the other! There were even fitted wardrobes with our initials on them, so now it was definitely the best house ever! I have such happy memories of living there.

We lived there for five years after Aaron arrived, but even though I loved it, there was a lot of work that needed to be done on the house, so when I was ten we moved to Wigmore. At first I was *so* upset, absolutely gutted; when I say 'at first', I think I was gutted for about four years! Initially I said I wanted to go and live with my friend who was still near to the old house. The house we moved to was a good twenty-minute walk from the same high school, so it was more travel, and I really missed playing out with my friends from the old place. It was a big wrench. Eventually I settled in and started to enjoy myself again.

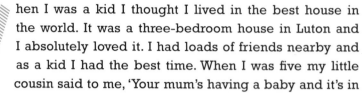

Mum and Dad were always working hard. Mum worked in various offices and Dad has always been involved in car manufacturing, which is a big industry around Luton. Mum worked for years at a newsagent's called Hendersons, which was great. In fact, it's so good that all of us have had jobs there over the years! I worked there for about six months in my early twenties.

We still live in the 'new' house and now I am older I can see this is a much better area than before. It's a really nice place, there's no trouble, it's our own little world. In my early twenties I moved out to a flat in Luton town centre, but I just wanted to go back to Wigmore; everyone just loves it round here.

Primary School for me was Putteridge. I loved it. I felt it was the best school in the world, especially the infant school. My head teacher, Mr Morton (who has sadly died), was brilliant. Everybody knew and respected him and he really turned that school into something special. The lessons were great; the teachers were fantastic. I was very good at reading and was always in the top class for that, and I look back on my time at school with fond memories. That said, while I knew the importance of classes and working hard, I was always sure of what I wanted to do for my career: it was all about singing.

'ALTHOUGH NOBODY BEFORE ME HAD PERFORMED PROFESSIONALLY IN ANY WAY, ALMOST THE ENTIRE FAMILY DID SHOWS, AMATEUR DRAMATICS, MUSICALS AND SO ON. MY MUM WAS A DANCER AND HAD TRAINED TO BE A DANCE TEACHER WHEN SHE WAS YOUNGER. MY MUM IS ALSO A BRILLIANT SINGER, MY NAN ALWAYS SANG OPERA AND MY UNCLE HAS A GREAT VOICE TOO, SO I WAS ALWAYS ENCOURAGED TO SING, PERFORM AND BE INVOLVED IN SHOWS.'

I can clearly remember the very first time I stood up in front of people and sang. I was in a choir and we had to sing in front of everyone and when it came to my turn I just loved it. It felt like the most natural thing in the world for me to do. I guess you can trace some of that back to my family. Although nobody before me had performed professionally in any way, almost the entire family did shows, amateur dramatics, musicals and so on. My mum was a dancer and had trained to be a dance teacher when she was younger. My mum is also a brilliant singer, my nan always sang opera and my uncle has a great voice too, so I was always encouraged to sing, perform and be involved in shows. At a very young age I used to go to old people's homes with my family, who had formed this little show group, and we'd sing to the residents.

I was in as many school plays as I could manage, but for some reason I never got the lead! There was always this one boy who seemed to get the lead every time. I was frustrated but I just wanted to be involved so I still loved taking part. I did a lot of after-school clubs as well, such as gymnastics. I was quite good at that. And, of course, I went to see loads of shows with my family in the West End and locally. When I was around six I also started attending a Saturday-morning drama school, and I would always join the summer clubs and holiday schools too in order to learn as much about performing as I could.

Whenever I sang alongside friends of a similar age, I could hear something different – I know that might sound arrogant and I really don't want it to! – but what I am trying to say is that I could hear I had a big range in my voice. Even back then I could really belt it out. I knew I could sing. This just encouraged me even more.

As I'd started showing an intense interest in performing from a very young age, my family encouraged me even more; they could see I really meant business. It is unusual for boys to excel at dramatics and performing; the most common route is to be really into football and sport, but I hated all that. It just wasn't for me. I just wanted to sing. Don't get me wrong, I wasn't thinking, *This is what I want to do as a job*, I just knew I loved singing and performing and I felt so at home and happy when I was doing that. Conversely, I knew I didn't want to be a vet or a doctor. At that age I never really lived in what you would call a 'normal' realm. In my head it was all about singing, performing, dressing up and make-believe with my toys. I enjoyed living in this little world of my own. So throughout my early school years I took part in plays and sang with my family whenever I could, but it was at high school that my singing really took off.

'AT THAT AGE I NEVER REALLY LIVED IN WHAT YOU WOULD CALL A 'NORMAL' REALM. IN MY HEAD IT WAS ALL ABOUT SINGING, PERFORMING, DRESSING UP AND MAKE-BELIEVE WITH MY TOYS. I ENJOYED LIVING IN THIS LITTLE WORLD OF MY OWN. SO THROUGHOUT MY EARLY SCHOOL YEARS I TOOK PART IN PLAYS AND SANG WITH MY FAMILY WHENEVER I COULD, BUT IT WAS AT HIGH SCHOOL THAT MY SINGING REALLY TOOK OFF.'

I was so excited to get to high school because of one teacher in particular, Mr Ridout. He was just the most amazing music teacher. I owe all of what has happened to me since – including with Union J – to him, without a shadow of a doubt. He was my nan's choirmaster and he'd also helped my cousins who had been to the school before me. Everyone always spoke so highly of Mr Ridout, so I was really excited about going to this school just to be in his class.

Initially I realised there were loads of other kids who were really talented at high school, and who could sing and dance and act very well. But that didn't put me off; it just made me feel like I had to bring my A game and prove that I was the best. There was definitely an air of competition locally, to see who was the best, and I loved that. I wanted to be the best.

It is high school that holds the clearest memories of my early singing for me. In the very first term I had to sing in front of the whole year in assembly. Just like that time at primary school it felt like the most natural thing in the world to do. At first some of the kids were taking the mick, everyone thought I'd quietly sing some little song, but instead I belted out Celine Dion's 'My Heart Will Go On'! As my performance went on I started to get some confidence in me and I stood there looking at all my school mates, thinking, *No one else here has got a voice like this. I can do this.* Obviously it was unusual for a boy to be belting out female songs like that. It's a lovely memory because I remember smashing it.

I started to soak up all sorts of influences in my singing. I worked hard in class and also made the most of every opportunity outside of the convential subjects to improve my singing. In Year Seven I joined a choir and that taught me so much. I was still going to the local drama school and they were brilliant. They were forever telling all the kids there that they were amazing. I owe a lot to them, not least because those were my formative days. Around this time my uncle moved to Spain and we would sometimes visit him, and when we did I'd have a go at the karaoke nights. I loved doing that. I'd sing all the Celine songs, Whitney, Mariah – all the big female ballad singers. I never sang male songs; I didn't need to and I didn't want to.

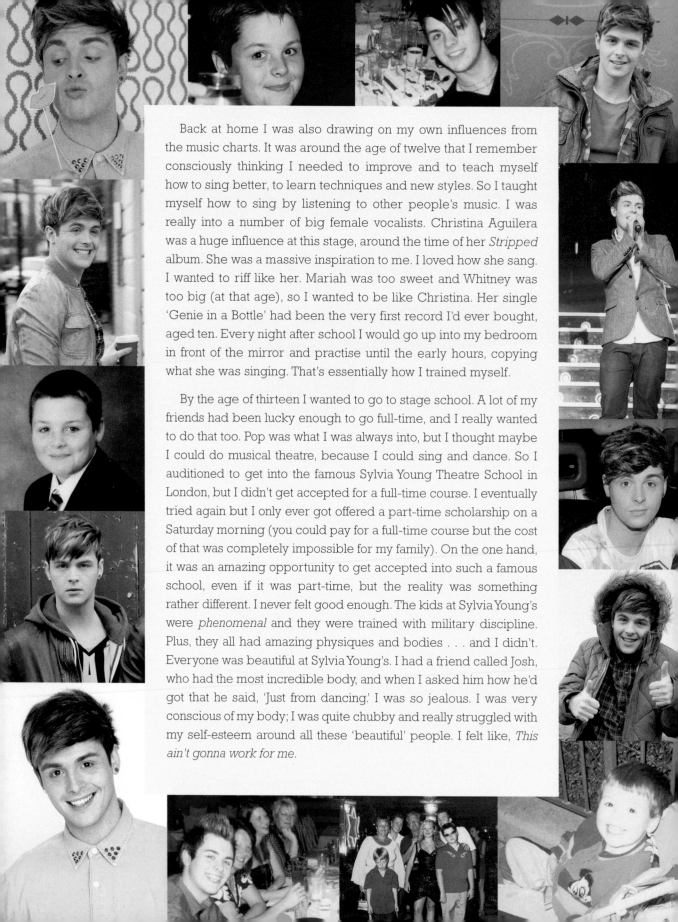

Back at home I was also drawing on my own influences from the music charts. It was around the age of twelve that I remember consciously thinking I needed to improve and to teach myself how to sing better, to learn techniques and new styles. So I taught myself how to sing by listening to other people's music. I was really into a number of big female vocalists. Christina Aguilera was a huge influence at this stage, around the time of her *Stripped* album. She was a massive inspiration to me. I loved how she sang. I wanted to riff like her. Mariah was too sweet and Whitney was too big (at that age), so I wanted to be like Christina. Her single 'Genie in a Bottle' had been the very first record I'd ever bought, aged ten. Every night after school I would go up into my bedroom in front of the mirror and practise until the early hours, copying what she was singing. That's essentially how I trained myself.

By the age of thirteen I wanted to go to stage school. A lot of my friends had been lucky enough to go full-time, and I really wanted to do that too. Pop was what I was always into, but I thought maybe I could do musical theatre, because I could sing and dance. So I auditioned to get into the famous Sylvia Young Theatre School in London, but I didn't get accepted for a full-time course. I eventually tried again but I only ever got offered a part-time scholarship on a Saturday morning (you could pay for a full-time course but the cost of that was completely impossible for my family). On the one hand, it was an amazing opportunity to get accepted into such a famous school, even if it was part-time, but the reality was something rather different. I never felt good enough. The kids at Sylvia Young's were *phenomenal* and they were trained with military discipline. Plus, they all had amazing physiques and bodies . . . and I didn't. Everyone was beautiful at Sylvia Young's. I had a friend called Josh, who had the most incredible body, and when I asked him how he'd got that he said, 'Just from dancing.' I was so jealous. I was very conscious of my body; I was quite chubby and really struggled with my self-esteem around all these 'beautiful' people. I felt like, *This ain't gonna work for me*.

Sylvia's really knocked me back. I went from being one of the best kids locally to being quite average. Looking back, that realisation could have killed my ambition massively. They were *so* good and *so* talented. It was unreal how good they were. It wasn't just the singing either; there was a focus on dancing and acting too. My main instrument was always the voice. Dancing I was fine with; in fact, I'd say I was a quick learner and I did enjoy those classes. But I wasn't at all confident at acting, so that sapped my confidence even more.

BUT I AM NOTHING IF NOT A FIGHTER, SO THERE WAS AN ODD CONTRADICTION DURING MY TIME AT SYLVIA YOUNG'S. ON THE ONE HAND I WAS VERY MUCH INTIMIDATED BY THESE BEAUTIFUL, TALENTED PEOPLE, BUT ON THE OTHER HAND I WOULD NOT LET THAT STOP ME.

I knew I could sing and I knew I could make something of myself, so even though it knocked my confidence I was determined not to let it get in my way. I will always stand up and fight for something I believe in. So despite my physical awkwardness, despite my nerves around having to act, and despite the standard being so intimidating I refused to be put off and I *made* myself improve. I quite literally pulled myself up to a higher standard; I put the hours in and I never gave up. I just kept telling myself, even in the darkest moments of self-doubt, *No, this will not beat me. I have got to practise and learn, and not stop until I am better than these kids.* I felt I had talent and I was so driven to make that work for me.

Gradually my confidence started to creep back and I began to enjoy myself more. There was one morning when we were in singing class and I was asked to stand up with two girls and perform 'Wind Beneath My Wings', most famously sung by Bette Midler. I absolutely belted that song out and I clearly remember kids were stopping in the corridor and looking in through the windows, trying to see who it was!

Although I found the talent at Sylvia Young's intimidating, I knew this world – singing, entertaining, performing – was for me. I knew I belonged there. Part of that was because of the open and wonderfully accepting attitudes in showbusiness. Why would that appeal to me? Because when I was fourteen I had my first boyfriend. I told my parents that I was gay because I have never been about hiding anything, and so telling them was easy in the sense that it was just who I was. They were fantastic; my mum seemed to already know and they have both never been anything other than fantastic.

I never really had a conversation with my mum about it; we had a mutual understanding, and it was never ever gonna be a problem. She is a massive influence in my life. She has always pushed me and she is a very strong person who a lot of people look up to. So to be able to have that support from her was incredible. My whole family were brilliant.

At Sylvia Young's there were other kids who were openly gay and proudly so, and that made me feel like this was a place I needed to be. Because of coming out and finding out about my sexuality, I felt an affinity with so many of these kids. *I need to be in this world.* Singing and being gay were synonymous for me, they were both an integral part of me growing up and still are. Being gay made me different and my love of singing did too, and I thrived on that.

During my mid-teens I was also trying to find out about myself as a singer and performer. As I told you earlier, I was big into Christina and other female vocalists, and initially my ability to sing like that was considered unusual for a boy. However, as you develop and grow older, that sort of mimicry is actually a disadvantage, because in order to progress to the highest level you need to have your *own* voice, and your own distinctive style and personality.

'I TOLD MY PARENTS THAT I WAS GAY BECAUSE I HAVE NEVER BEEN ABOUT HIDING ANYTHING, AND SO TELLING THEM WAS EASY IN THE SENSE THAT IT WAS JUST WHO I WAS. THEY WERE FANTASTIC; MY MUM SEEMED TO ALREADY KNOW AND THEY HAVE BOTH NEVER BEEN ANYTHING OTHER THAN FANTASTIC.'

Sounding too much like Christina or Britney is not going to work in your favour in the long-term. For a good while I was doing too much mimicking, so I never really knew who I was. Mimicking is a useful tool – I have always learnt by mimicking, whether it's learning to sing, play the piano, trumpet, violin, drums, or whatever. I have never read music, so my only route was to listen to a singer and copy what they were doing. But at some point you need to develop your own voice.

Ironically, looking back, I actually think that I wouldn't be doing Union J if I had got a full-time scholarship at Sylvia Young's. A lot of the kids who go there full-time end up seeing it all as work – and it is hard work; this isn't a hobby – and sometimes that puts people off and they don't pursue it as a career. For me, Saturdays were enough.

By now I was obsessed with singing. I was going to be a singer, that was what I was programmed to do, I told myself. It was a pivotal time because this was also the first time I'd really noticed *X Factor*. When I turned sixteen I went along and auditioned, but I didn't get past the first stage.

That year, a young female singer broke through on the show, who only fuelled my obsession with singing: Leona Lewis. When she won *X Factor* I was completely blown away by her. I remember thinking, *God, this girl is incredible.* I was obsessed with Leona, obsessed! During this period I spent hour after hour training my voice completely by hers. Leona also had another significant effect: she made me realise I wanted to be a pop star, rather than stay in musical theatre.

In 2006 I started BRIT School in London. My friend Tiffany had managed to get in there and it was free – you didn't need money to get in, you just had to audition and be talented. So I thought, *I should do that.* Some of the other stage schools were charging upwards of £30,000 a year, which was out of the question obviously. But BRIT wasn't like that. I was already heavily into the idea of going when I found out that Leona Lewis had gone there, and that was it: my mind was made up!

I felt some of the other stage schools were a bit snooty (not Sylvia's I must point out!), and you looked a certain way, you danced a certain way. By contrast, BRIT was a bit like the odd-job school. The fat kids, the gay kids, the geeks, the self-taught, the alternatives. It really was like *Fame*. I knew I would be in my element there. I love individuals! For example, I love big girls that dance; I love girls who shave their heads; boys that dress in drag; I love people who don't look how they 'should'; I love quirky, weird, unusual people. Anyone who has something *different*! That should only ever be celebrated! BRIT seemed to encourage this individuality.

My best friend, Alice, is an amazing actress and she wanted to go to BRIT as well, so we both decided to audition. You needed to get good grades at school, they were keen on that, so that was an incentive for me

to concentrate in class for once. By this point I hated schoolwork. It just wasn't for me. I never did my homework. In fact, I am surprised I passed anything! But I did knuckle down when I thought it might affect my chances of getting into BRIT.

So I went and auditioned and performed a song from *Les Mis*. I'd previously been in a local production of the musical in the role of Marius, so I was very familiar with the piece and I think I smashed it. That was my big musical-theatre song; it was very belty and dramatic, so I sang that and thankfully it went really well. Then I had to do a dance audition and that went okay, but when it came to the acting audition I hated it. It was cringeworthy, monologue-ing in front of all these kids who wanted to be professional actors and who were well read on acting techniques and all that. It was just awful. I kept thinking, *I am dying on my arse here!* Alice came a few weeks later to audition and hers went so much better than mine, so I was really pleased for her. Then around my birthday I was at school when Mum rang and said I'd had a letter from BRIT. She opened it and then told me the most amazing news . . . I was in!

At that moment I thought to myself, *Life is going to change. I am going to the most amazing stage school in London. I am off!* I knew my life had changed forever. I felt like a bit of a hotshot, like I really meant business. The only sad part was that Alice didn't get in, which was a real shame. It was so sad, we were supposed to be going together.

I remember my first day at BRIT. It really was so different. Everyone was so different. The alternative kids were *really* alternative, and I was like, *This is AMAZING!* You are encouraged to be yourself, to be creative, to think differently, so everyone was on top of their game. I had all these talented people around me and I thrived on that.

When I first started BRIT the vibrato in my voice was really thin and shaky. I loved Leona and her deep, prominent vibrato was incredible. I must have listened to her version of 'Over the Rainbow' from the live shows about a million times. I wanted her voice!

There were noticeboards around the school where people pinned up posters for auditions and opportunities. Just before the first Christmas I spotted a notice about an audition for a boy band and – being so naive at this stage – I thought to myself, *Ha ha! I will go for that, I will get in and the band will be massive. That's me done!* So I auditioned for the first round in this classroom at the school and I got through; then the next round they took us into a recording studio to sing, but after that they phoned me up and said I hadn't got through. I was gutted. This was supposed to be my chance. This was how I was going to make it! That was my first adult rejection and it blew me away. I was like, *NO! This is not happening!*

'I HAD PRETTY MUCH DECIDED THAT I COULDN'T LEAVE BRIT BUT THEN I GOT THIS PHONE CALL TO SAY THE BAND WAS GOING TO SUPPORT WESTLIFE ON A NATIONAL ARENA TOUR FOR THE LOVE ALBUM! THIS WAS RIDICULOUS: THE STUFF OF MY DREAMS.'

After I'd brushed myself down I kept searching for boy-band auditions and I was more determined than ever. Another one came along quickly, so I signed up for that. I had to go to Pineapple Dance Studios in central London, and when I got there I joined a queue with about thirty other boys. The band in question was looking for a replacement member and I'd done my research and found out that they'd previously performed 'Hello' by Lionel Ritchie, so in my audition I sang that. I went in and belted it out. God knows what I looked like . . . Well, I do know actually. I looked awful; I've got the pictures! Somehow I got through the first round and in the second there were only three of us left. We performed again and then they sat me down and said, 'You've got it. You are in the band!'

We were called Code 5. I was ecstatic. As far as I was concerned this was going to be the next Spice Girls, so I couldn't believe what I was hearing. This was major. In my head I was like, *Oh my God, I am literally gonna make it now. All my dreams will come true!* Naive!

There was a problem, though – it wasn't clear if I could do this and still attend BRIT because I wouldn't have the time to do both. I was really scared; what the hell was I gonna do? I had pretty much decided that I couldn't leave BRIT but then I got this phone call to say the band was going to support Westlife on a national arena tour for *The Love Album!* This was ridiculous: the stuff of my dreams.

I did some drama exams on the Monday morning and then, having told no one except my mum, I walked out of college, straight to the train station and off on tour with Westlife, one of the biggest boy bands of all time. I didn't tell a soul where I was going. And I felt so liberated. I felt like, *THIS IS IT! I am going to be a superstar!* So I got on the train to Derby to meet the tour manager, who informed us that we had to find a fifth member in just a week, so we auditioned all these boys at a studio, chose one and then had a week to practise before the tour.

I eventually told BRIT, and they said they couldn't be certain my place would still be there when I came back off tour. That was a risk I was willing to take and, looking back, it was a stupid, stupid risk. But at the time, as you can imagine, this was all very exciting. I was seventeen and touring the country in all the big arenas!

And, yes, the tour was amazing. We played some massive venues, and I got to sing at Wembley Arena, which very few people of that age have done – it was incredible. All my friends and family came to watch me at Wembley. Six months after I had left high school in Luton my life had completely changed. I remember flying back to go to a staff do at a local gay bar, where I worked collecting glasses. I was telling people how it was all going on tour and they were amazed that I had 'flown in' for this night out, like I was some big superstar. I think I paid forty quid for a Ryanair flight! Ha ha!

Then that all came crashing down massively. I started to feel I was underappreciated in the band, pushed to the back because I was youngest, and the other guys were singing lead because of the way they looked. They were lovely-looking and had great bodies, but I felt they couldn't sing like I could. And over time that really wound me up. I'll be honest, I kicked off a little bit. I have always had a hot head and can be a bit of a pain in the arse if I believe what I am fighting for; if I am standing up for something, there's no one to tell me I am wrong. I felt like saying, 'Yes, I am gay. Yes, I am a bit chubby but I can still be lead!' It became apparent that this wasn't going to work and eventually I parted ways with the band.

Fortunately for me, my place was still there at BRIT, but it was actually really hard to get back into. I had been on tour with Westlife so I kind of came back down to earth with a bang. But I picked myself up and worked hard and finished the year, gaining a National Diploma in Performing Arts.

After BRIT my life was a bit crap and reality hit. I had no job, no university course to aim for, no singing opportunities, no nothing. And that was my life for five years!

Don't get me wrong, I kept auditioning constantly, for this band and that, but nothing was working out. I would sometimes look back and think I had missed my chance and it was really easy to get very demoralised. There was such a long time when nothing worked out for me. I guess I just coasted for five years . . .

One thing that kept tempting me, though, was *X Factor*. I'd auditioned that time before BRIT, then again after Code 5 had toured with Westlife, and actually got to the judges' auditions on TV in 2007 but didn't get through. That knocked me massively because it felt like a door had opened up momentarily and then – like every other door at the time – was slammed in my face. I even set up my own band to get on *X Factor* but that didn't work out either. Eventually I would audition for the show five times, but until 2012 nothing worked.

I needed to earn money and so I took a job singing at a holiday camp, but I really didn't enjoy it. It was hard graft singing covers in front of forty holidaymakers every night but I still had to earn money, so after this I would also work in shops and bars, as well as teaching dancing and singing part-time. But I never held down one particular job for long.

It was a really hard time. I persevered, though; I tried every single avenue I could find: every competition, every audition, every chance to earn money singing. I got myself an agent, booked gigs at a lot of the gay clubs where I would warm up for drag queens. I really worked the gay scene. I also recorded some songs that were put forward for a gay dance album and I did the Pride festival. But time after time these new 'opportunities' came to nothing. I actually started to think, *Maybe this could just be a dream forever?* I began to doubt my self-belief every day; I felt I was meant to do this but there had been so many rejections in that lengthy barren spell that my spirit had started to dwindle. When it's five years ago that you toured with Westlife and nothing has happened since, you really do start to doubt yourself and your dream. The excitement of life on the road and being a pop band seemed like a distant memory.

I HAD HAD ENOUGH.

I FELT SO DEJECTED AND I WAS TIRED OF BEING TOLD 'NO'. AND YET SOMETHING IN ME WANTED TO GIVE THIS ONE FINAL SHOT.

I HEARD ABOUT AN AUDITION FOR A NEW BOY BAND SO I DECIDED TO GIVE IT ONE LAST GO . . .

JOSH CUTHBERT

When I was five I lived in a three-storey pink house in Singapore. That might seem strange for a Camberley boy, but it was because my dad had taken up a job in IT overseas, so we all moved there for a few years. I had been born in Portsmouth but I don't have many memories of my time there before we moved to south-east Asia. Sadly, after a while over there, my parents split up and so I moved back to England with my mum, while Dad had to stay in Singapore for work. He would always fly back for birthdays and big events so I still got to see him as much as possible.

Although I was too young to recall many feelings, I do remember the split being quite tough, but after some time my mum met a wonderful guy called Graham, who is now my stepdad. He came along and really looked after us; he would take us on wonderful holidays, make sure we had everything we needed and just generally was amazing. It was incredible growing up with him and there is now a real bond between us. At the time that really helped me – my dad will always be my dad, but having a father figure as brilliant as Graham around when I didn't see my own dad much did help. He had two children with Mum – Callum and Victoria – and we had the most amazing times growing up as brothers and sisters. (Callum is now a brilliant teenage lad and Victoria is eleven going on twenty-two, a really lovely girl.)

Back in Singapore my dad then met a lovely lady called Alison; she is amazing and they now have two kids, Lucy and Sophie, who are twins. Why do I tell you all this? Because while it might have felt unsettling to a young lad, I now feel so lucky because I have the most amazing extended family! It's great. I've got brothers and sisters, all these nans and grandads. It's just such a loving and brilliant family to be a part of. I don't look at any of them as stepbrothers or sisters; they are just my family. I even call my stepdad's mum 'Nanny' – she's not actually, but she is in my eyes. That side of the family treat me no differently to their own kids, from day one they have been lovely. I think everything happens for a reason and I couldn't feel luckier; those difficult times have actually enriched my life with so much more love, which is incredible.

We lived back in Portsmouth for a couple of years and then relocated to Winkfield in Berkshire, in between Ascot and Windsor. I feel like I have grown up in Ascot, so that is where I class as home, a hundred per cent. Happily by then I would see my real dad every other weekend as he'd relocated back to England, and as the years have gone on that relationship has been brilliant too.

School for me was Cranbourne Primary, which was really small, with only about fifty kids in each year. It was a lovely building filled with really nice teachers – awesome. Right from a very young age, football was my passion and, in particular, Chelsea! I am a huge fan, *huge*! Both my dad and stepdad are also Blues fans so it is in my blood. Graham has had a season ticket for thirty years and we would regularly go down to the match.

Being completely honest, my boyhood dream was to be a footballer. I played in local under-ten teams at first and gradually worked my way up the ladder as I grew older and gained more confidence and ability. Eventually I had a stint of being captain. My main football memories are playing for Ascot United; I spent so much time down that training ground, working hard and playing all the time. There'd be matches at weekends and in the week, training on this AstroTurf pitch, and rocking up in the cold winter months with my little shin pads sticking to me in the freezing cold, our parents taking it in turns to ferry all these muddy kids around the area. My manager down at Ascot United, Phil Reece, took me from a ten-year-old kid right through to the adult leagues, and because I was down there so much, he became a big part of my life. I have such fond memories of those times – the matches, the excitement, the team spirit – and I miss that a lot. I love working as a team; there is no better feeling than winning something or achieving something with your best mates around you – a feeling I would later experience on a whole new level when Union J took off.

Back to my early years: by the age of twelve I was being watched by talent scouts for professional football clubs, such as Reading and West Ham, and I would eventually go on to have trials for both these teams. I've never hidden the fact that football has always been a passion. My obsession is quite extreme! I love my football.

Secondary school was Charters in Sunningdale; it was a really good sports school. I enjoyed my time there, but there were a few years when I was often on report, getting sent out and even refusing to do what the teachers asked of me. It happened quite a lot in science. The teacher would get fed up with my behaviour and finally snap and shout, 'Josh, get out!' And I would just go, 'No!' So she'd say it again, 'Get out!' and I'd just give her cheek back. Meanwhile, the whole class would be killing themselves laughing, and there I was thinking I was really cool (when, in fact, I know now it was stupid), so then she'd call for back-up and the head of science would come and go, 'Josh, get out!' Same reply: 'No!' But they'd always win because they knew I was terrified of the Head of Year, so they'd call him and when he'd say, 'Josh, get out!' I'd go, 'Yes, sir. Sorry, sir,' and walk out! I did stupid stuff: setting off the fire alarms, causing problems in class; silly, immature behaviour. I look back on that and think, *Why did you do that?*

In my defence, I wasn't naughty all the time, and, in fact, the teachers often sent reports home saying that I was a lovely boy but I was just a bit of a class clown. I suppose I concentrated too much on making other people laugh, rather than getting on with my work.

My mum helped a lot; she was really patient and thoughtful about how to make my situation improve. I vividly remember how she came up with this reward scheme where I would get treats if I could get praise in every lesson for a certain period of time, perhaps a week or so. 'Effort 1' was the top score so I'd go home with this report card and if there were enough 'Effort 1' marks on there I might get say ten pounds or a Chelsea ticket or whatever. It's funny what sticks in your mind but I can clearly recall one week when I had been doing really well: I'd got to Thursday and I was getting praise all the time but then for some reason I let it slip and the last day was a write-off. I sat dejected on the bus home with a half-empty bottle of Tippex, trying to blank out the collection of poor 'Effort 3' marks I'd managed to earn at the last minute. It worked and my mum never knew (sorry, Mum!), but they must have rumbled me because shortly after they changed the report cards to yellow, so my Tippex was useless!

I was quite late starting to be interested in girls and all that stuff. I am quite insecure and I think that was one of the reasons. I was insecure looks-wise (even now as an adult this is still the case), and back then I was a little bit chubby and I always wanted to be in the cool group but I was just not quite there. That was quite hard and I think I swerved round that by trying to make people laugh instead.

Charters is a big school, so there were 125 girls in my year, and there were five or six girls that I really fancied, like most boys that age. My favourite was a girl in my science class but I was too self-conscious and awkward around her to make any kind of move. Then one day the teacher suddenly put us together in the new seating plan, which was great! I started to grow up and lose some weight around this time too and feel a little bit more confident, so we got close, but nothing really serious.

I suppose that's why I was a bit of a nightmare at school, because I was more worried about impressing girls and other boys, trying to get in the cool group and all that rubbish – stuff that you look back on and know is garbage but at the time seemed so very important. My best two friends at school were Ryan Rocastle and James Mitchell and they still are to this day. I'm proud to say that I never wanted to be in the 'cool' group enough to smoke. To this day I've never smoked. I have no interest in that whatsoever and I never saw that as cool in any way. Whatever!

At this age football was still everything to me. I played football locally and kept really fit, I had those trials at Reading and played there for eighteen months, then I had trials for West Ham too, plus I was scouted for QPR. My local team in Ascot was really good and a lot of quality players came from there, so scouts were always sniffing around.

In terms of singing I did actually start from a relatively early age, the last year of primary at Cranbourne, in fact. My first clear memory of performing

'I WAS QUITE LATE STARTING TO BE INTERESTED IN GIRLS AND ALL THAT STUFF. I AM QUITE INSECURE AND I THINK THAT WAS ONE OF THE REASONS. I WAS INSECURE LOOKS-WISE (EVEN NOW AS AN ADULT THIS IS STILL THE CASE), AND BACK THEN I WAS A LITTLE BIT CHUBBY AND I ALWAYS WANTED TO BE IN THE COOL GROUP BUT I WAS JUST NOT QUITE THERE. THAT WAS QUITE HARD AND I THINK I SWERVED ROUND THAT BY TRYING TO MAKE PEOPLE LAUGH INSTEAD.'

was at the Christmas play. No one had a clue that I could sing; I didn't really have a clue that I could hold a note myself! But I thought I was okay, so I decided to put myself forward for the main role in *Scrooge*. When the teacher asked if anyone wanted to sing for the main part I put my hand up. She was really shocked and said, 'Are you sure, Josh?', but I was adamant so I stood up and everyone went silent when I started singing. It was a really weird feeling. And then, to my amazement, I got the main part!

On the night of the performance all my family came to watch me and they had no idea that I could sing. I didn't sing around the house or anything; it was all about football as far as they were concerned. As soon as Mum saw that show, she said, 'We have to get you to stage school, Josh!' She was really excited.

So I started going to a Stagecoach every Saturday morning before football. At first it took a lot of persuasion for me to do that, mainly because I thought, *I am a boy! I am a footballer! Should I be dancing and singing and acting?* Anyway, I soon realised I loved it and I improved really quickly. After just a few months, they put me forward for an audition for *Chitty Chitty Bang Bang* at the London Palladium, so I went along, auditioned and somehow got the part! This was less than two years after I'd first stood up in class for that audition for *Scrooge*.

Suddenly I was rehearsing on this huge stage in the West End with people like Christopher Biggins, Jason Donovan, Brian Conley and Stephen Gately. Yet all the 'training' I'd really had was just those Saturday mornings at Stagecoach, which to be honest were really light-hearted, no pressure. You just went along and had a good time. I can remember the first night of *Chitty Chitty Bang Bang* like it was yesterday. I think I was close to dribbling, I was that scared. Since a lot of the cast were very young, we had to spend ages in rehearsals but, even so, when it came to the opening show there were a lot of nerves. I was Head Sewer Child, one of about twenty kids like that, and when I made my entrance I had to crawl under this metal bar out into the open, but I somehow got my trousers stuck and as I pulled forward they ripped all along from my thigh down to my shin. I was really scared but I just carried on, and I guess as I was supposed to be living in a sewer no one really noticed! Photos from the performances show me as this chubby kid with cheeks the size of a table, covered in all this dark make-up.

The performances were brilliant fun and I did that for nine months, but my overriding memory of that show was the amazing times I would spend with my grandma. Every single Thursday and Friday she would pick me up from Mum's after school, I'd have a little snack and then she'd take me to Slough train station. She'd drop me off and I'd run in and queue for the tickets while she parked the car, then we'd hop on the train to Paddington, then the underground to Oxford Circus for the theatre.

Grandma would then buy herself a ticket; she had to pay every time! She'd often wait at the box office for the last remaining tickets so she could get the cheaper ones. She'd always be right at the front, which at that theatre were actually quite bad seats because they were almost too close. I would come on stage and immediately look for her. I'd always see her and that was an amazing feeling. She was so proud. After the show she would wait for me to remove the make-up and get dressed, then we would have some dinner and head home. I loved going up into town with her and I got really, really close with her during that period.

I'm lucky because my mum came dozens of times too! She was so proud as well. My family have always been so supportive. I've never been lonely in terms of singing and following my dream. Mum came to every audition; she would take days off work even when it was really inconvenient. She was – and is – incredible and I've probably actually got a lot more to thank her for than I realise.

It wasn't just singing that I was doing reasonably well at, I also started to get small parts in other projects too. I was in a four-minute anti-bullying campaign film that got sent to thousands of schools across the country . . . but the problem was in the film itself I was the bully! I would always be involved in some play at school too, so I was really busy. I also left Stagecoach and started going to Sylvia Young's Theatre School in London, which was absolutely brilliant. I only went on the Saturday and I wasn't especially into all the dancing (although I liked street dance), but I really enjoyed it and through their agency I found out about even more auditions for shows like *Oliver!* and stuff like that. So I was gaining experience all the time. Once again, my mum was always there, for every single audition and performance, which thinking back is a lot of money, time and energy.

Meanwhile at school, I did turn it round as I got older and by the time I'd got to my GCSEs I had really knuckled down and actually enjoyed my education. I had a whale of a time. Something just seemed to click in my head and I was a completely different person. The whole singing part of my life was running in parallel with my continued obsession with football. Unfortunately, the latter was about to be knocked sideways when I suffered a horrific injury one New Year's Eve.

I am a goalkeeper and, although I am quite tall now, at that point I was just average in height, which can be a disadvantage. I made up for that by being very agile and brave, so I would throw myself into any challenge and leap all over the place. I was what they call a shot stopper. Anyway, I was at my step-grandad's house one New Year's Eve and I was shooting an air rifle. I was putting a bullet in and when I cocked the rifle back it turned out to be faulty, and so it snapped back violently and chopped the end of my thumb off, including a chunk of the actual bone. It was just the most excruciating pain I have ever felt, and it was a pretty bloody sight too.

Luckily for me, we were just round the corner from a hospital in High Wycombe that had one of the best plastic-surgery units in the country, so I was rushed there. They operated on me and I had to spend the night in hospital – it kinda spoilt New Year's Eve! – but they did an amazing job and I am very thankful for that.

However, the reality was that I had lost the top part of my left thumb. This meant there was no chance of playing football for many months, not least because I was heavily bandaged up and the wound was quite severe and obviously not safe to play football with. I'd finished my trials at West Ham (which hadn't worked out) and now I had lost part of my thumb, so I couldn't play at all. I couldn't even use my Xbox or anything! And clearly I couldn't get acting roles or singing jobs because I had this massive bandage that couldn't be taken off! Eventually, after about six months of being completely out of action, I started to train lightly again, but at first even getting the goalie's glove on was an ordeal.

Over the next few months I gradually got back into playing local football, but something felt different. As much as I wanted to be the same as before the accident, I found it so hard. For one, the thumb really hurt. It was painful catching the ball and because I was playing at a high standard some of those guys could really belt their shots hard. Also, the nerve endings had all been mashed up, so if it was even slightly cold the pain was awful. Half the time I was trying to save shots with just my right hand. And finally, perhaps most terminally for my football career, my confidence had gone. I was getting scared in situations, whereas before the accident I would have instinctively been knee-deep in the action.

That was a really hard time. I was very self-conscious about the injury too, which didn't help. It's funny because now I am older and more self-assured, I don't noticeit any more. I kind of think it's unique to have something like that! I've never seen anyone with a chopped-off thumb and those kind of scars! It just makes me Josh.

I did slowly get back into my football and the thumb hurt less and less as it healed. I even got back to a high standard again and also started a refereeing course, running the touchline at adult games and refereeing junior games myself. And, of course, I started singing and performing again.

A year after *Chitty Chitty Bang Bang*, in 2007, they opened up *X Factor* for under-sixteens (it's now back at sixteen). I was so excited and my application was submitted in a heartbeat. I got through the first auditions and was sent to sing in front of the judges (Simon Cowell, Dannii Minogue, Louis Walsh and Sharon Osbourne) at the Emirates Stadium in north London. My whole family came – about forty people! It was lovely to see, because both Mum and Dad's side were there and everyone was chatting and getting on really well.

Back then there was no audience. You just went into a room with the four judges and film crew, and stood on the X and performed. I sang Frank Sinatra's 'Come Fly with Me', which was an odd choice because I'm not even sure my voice had dropped yet! However, I only got through two lines when Simon stopped me. I was so nervous already, so when he put his hand up I was just a wreck. He asked me if I had another song so I sang 'No Matter What' by Boyzone, who were my favourite band.

SHARON SAID I WAS 'ADORABLE' AND ALONG WITH DANNII GAVE ME A YES. LOUIS WAS BORDERLINE, BUT SIMON JUMPED AHEAD OF HIM AND SAID 'NO', SO IT WAS JUST DOWN TO BOYZONE'S MANAGER . . . AND EVENTUALLY HE SAID 'YES'! I COULD HAVE EXPLODED. I COULDN'T BELIEVE IT; I WAS THROUGH TO BOOTCAMP. I WALKED THROUGH THE DOOR AND ALL MY FAMILY JUMPED ON ME!

When I got to bootcamp (Mum had to come with me because of my young age) I was rejected as a solo singer, but then I got called back and had to go into this room with Simon Cowell, who sat me down and said he was putting me into a group called Young Hearts. That was all very exciting.

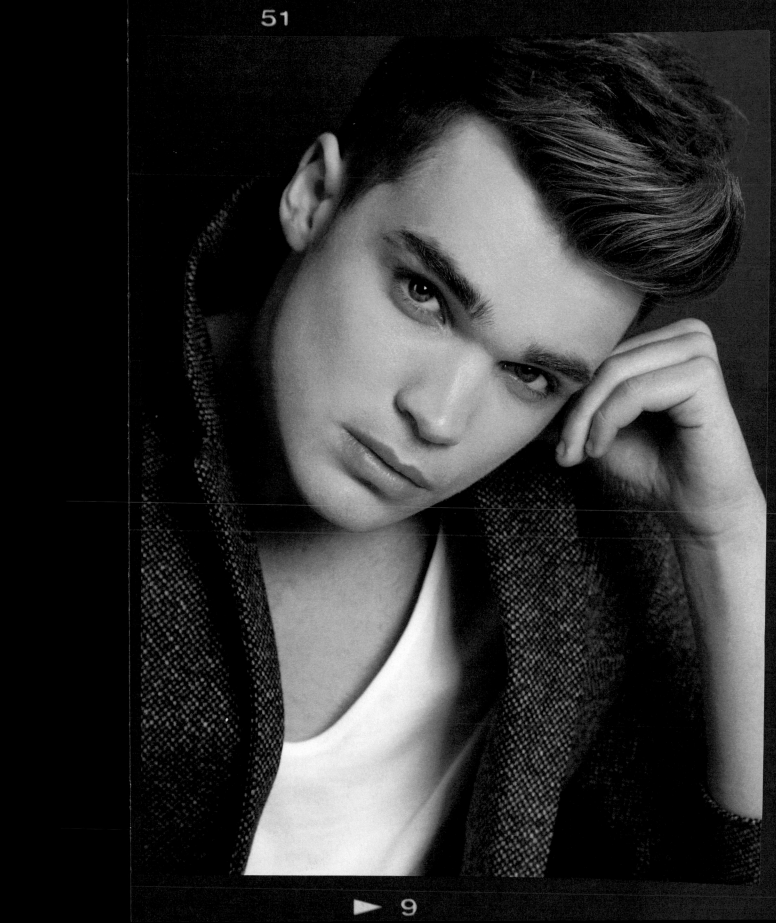

▶ 9

I met up with the rest of the band and it seemed like we were the focus of a lot of filming; the cameras seemed to follow us everywhere and we did loads of chatting and singing in front of the lens. So I thought there must be a reason for that: they want us in the show. But then we didn't get through. We did so much filming but nothing was shown. There are just a few random clips of me on my own, mainly looking upset. I was absolutely devastated.

I know it sounds a bit daft but the hardest thing was that people at school just didn't believe me. I'd said I was at bootcamp and I was being filmed all the time and they just thought I was a liar because none of it was shown. I thought I did really well for fifteen and, in fact, I was the youngest boy to do bootcamp at that point, but that didn't make it any easier going back to school. Having said all that, I really enjoyed the whole experience and even at the time I realised how much I wanted to sing as a career. So, for all the disappointment, it was a pivotal moment.

After that I was sharply focused on my singing career and I kept auditioning for parts and opportunities. About a year after *X Factor* I joined my first boy band, but that came to nothing, so when *X Factor* came round again I auditioned but this time didn't get put through at all. I started working with a guy in his mid-twenties who was in a great band called Fourth Base. Some of those guys had done *X Factor* a few years before and had even got to Judges' Houses, so for a while that was very exciting. I'd started college, doing Economics, English, History and Business Studies, but the band wanted me to concentrate on the group full-time. However, after much deliberation, I made the decision not to do that because I felt the band wasn't really going anywhere, so it fell apart for me soon after.

Next up, I got a call from a guy who worked for 19 Management and he said he had heard of me through a third party and would I like to go in and audition for a band that was looking to hook up with Universal Records. Now this was so exciting! Universal and 19 Management, these were major players, so I remember that phone call as one of the happiest moments of my life at that point (once again Mum came up to London with me).

In a couple of months they were talking about us moving into a house in London together. This was around the time that The Wanted were breaking through, so boy bands were all the talk again. It was a really exciting time.

Unfortunately, I didn't really get along with the band members much; to be fair, they were nice enough lads, and we had all been thrown together, but most of them were incredibly strong dancers, which I'm not. There was a very definite dance direction they wanted to go down and it just didn't feel right for me. I felt awkward. I knew what an incredible opportunity it was, but it just wasn't me. It took a lot for me to admit that to myself. I broke down in tears after one rehearsal because I wasn't as good as them at dancing and I remember ringing my mum afterwards and saying, 'I can't do this any more.' I knew I might be turning down the opportunity that I had looked for all these years, but it just felt wrong to stay in the band. I had big chats with my family about what to do. Eventually I made what was, looking back, quite a brave decision: I turned the band down and left. And, yes, for weeks, probably months, afterwards I couldn't help thinking, *What have I done?!*

Next I joined another band called Boulevard. I'd been approached on Facebook and the band flew over from Ireland to meet me. I ended up moving to Dublin for two months, so that was all very exciting for a while. Then we got the most amazing news: we had got a support slot touring with Boyzone! This was just incredible, this – surely? – was my chance to make it.

I need to stress at this point that Boyzone were my favourite band. I've always had a soft spot for boy bands, Westlife and Blue for example, but Boyzone were my number one. So to get this support slot was just ridiculous to me. I couldn't believe my luck. We played with them all over Ireland and in arenas in the UK, such as Sheffield. That was the first time I'd done anywhere near those sort of size venues. Just experiencing what a big tour was like was great fun. You met loads of girls and had great times with your band mates. It was amazing!

One afternoon while we were all waiting to soundcheck I went into the catering room and sat down on my own to grab a bite to eat. Out of the corner of my eye I spotted Ronan Keating walking across the room and then – as my heart started racing a million miles an hour – he sat down next to me at the table. I just froze. I remember thinking, *Do I have food stuck in my teeth?* Anyway, we had a little chat, and he was really nice and gave me all sorts of great advice about being in a band and the challenges of life on the road. He probably knew that we were never going to make it but he was really kind. He didn't have to go out of his way. They say 'Never meet your heroes' in case they let you down, but Ronan certainly didn't. It was a great feeling to know that he is such a nice guy.

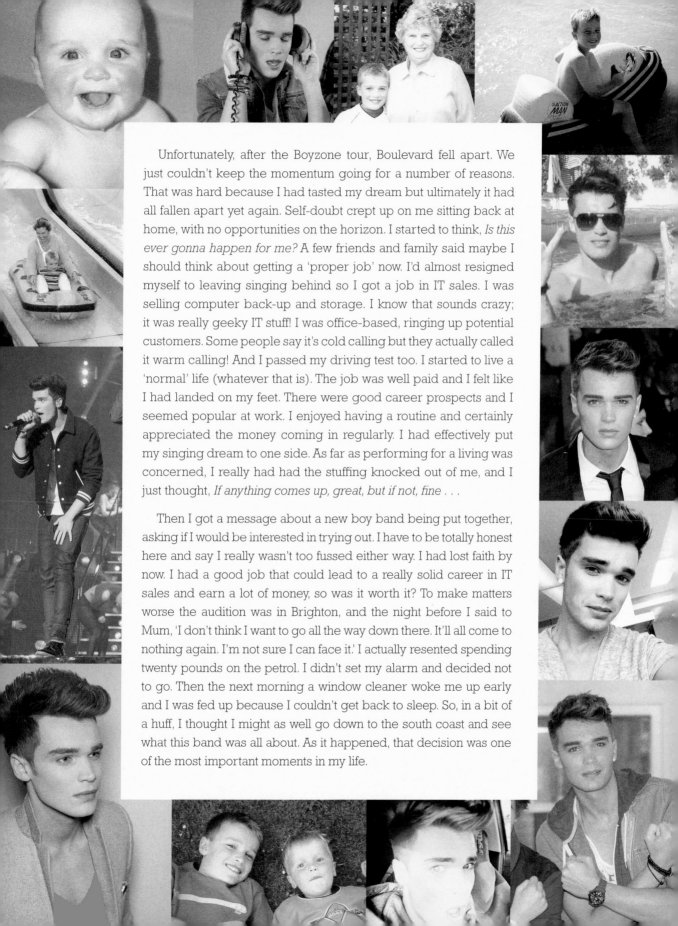

Unfortunately, after the Boyzone tour, Boulevard fell apart. We just couldn't keep the momentum going for a number of reasons. That was hard because I had tasted my dream but ultimately it had all fallen apart yet again. Self-doubt crept up on me sitting back at home, with no opportunities on the horizon. I started to think, *Is this ever gonna happen for me?* A few friends and family said maybe I should think about getting a 'proper job' now. I'd almost resigned myself to leaving singing behind so I got a job in IT sales. I was selling computer back-up and storage. I know that sounds crazy; it was really geeky IT stuff! I was office-based, ringing up potential customers. Some people say it's cold calling but they actually called it warm calling! And I passed my driving test too. I started to live a 'normal' life (whatever that is). The job was well paid and I felt like I had landed on my feet. There were good career prospects and I seemed popular at work. I enjoyed having a routine and certainly appreciated the money coming in regularly. I had effectively put my singing dream to one side. As far as performing for a living was concerned, I really had had the stuffing knocked out of me, and I just thought, *If anything comes up, great, but if not, fine . . .*

Then I got a message about a new boy band being put together, asking if I would be interested in trying out. I have to be totally honest here and say I really wasn't too fussed either way. I had lost faith by now. I had a good job that could lead to a really solid career in IT sales and earn a lot of money, so was it worth it? To make matters worse the audition was in Brighton, and the night before I said to Mum, 'I don't think I want to go all the way down there. It'll all come to nothing again. I'm not sure I can face it.' I actually resented spending twenty pounds on the petrol. I didn't set my alarm and decided not to go. Then the next morning a window cleaner woke me up early and I was fed up because I couldn't get back to sleep. So, in a bit of a huff, I thought I might as well go down to the south coast and see what this band was all about. As it happened, that decision was one of the most important moments in my life.

GEORGE SHELLEY

As kids, we kind of ruled the Shelley household! My mum was a single mum and for a variety of reasons we moved around a lot. Mum always let us have mates round to hang out and for sleepovers. When I say we moved around, it was literally every year or so at times. So, for example, I have lived in Clevedon, Nailsea, Taunton, Burnham-On-Sea, Backwell and Cheddar. I guess I think of Somerset as my home, because we always moved within that area.

My mum has had loads of different jobs. She trained to be a midwife, a nurse, a fitness instructor and a masseuse, so she was always busy. I've got two older brothers: William, who is four years older than me, and Tom, who is ten years older. Tom's got a different dad to me. In 1995, when I was two, my sister Harriet arrived, and I loved having her around. All the way through growing up it was just me, Mum, Harriet, William and Tom (who now lives in Australia). We would usually only have three bedrooms, so it would be me, Tom and William in one room. We were a really close-knit family and wherever we lived it was always a very busy, loud and hectic but fun house!

My dad met another lady called Row and they had children too (Leo, Archie, Spencer, Annabelle and Louisa), so those kids are now all a big part of my family as well. I love spending time with them all. So I was lucky. I had the Harrises in Bristol and the Shelleys living over in Nottingham, and we managed to see Dad as much as possible. Dad has been amazing; he has always pushed me to follow my instincts and make my own decisions and it is a highlight of my week whenever I get to see him!

Whenever we had mates round for massive sleepovers in the lounge Mum was always very relaxed about it and would join in the fun. She was a cool mum. I looked up to my Uncle Johnny a lot, my mum's brother. When I was little he was in a successful heavy metal alternative rock band called Sunna (with my other uncle, Tim, on drums), who had a major record deal with Virgin and were on MTV loads, so he was always off touring and recording albums. It was really exciting to be around him; he was my famous uncle. His boy, Sid (my cousin), was my best mate from when I was about five until my mid-teens. Me and Sid were constantly playing *Pokémon* or outside playing make-believe; we loved making up stories and acting them out.

'WE WOULD USUALLY ONLY HAVE THREE BEDROOMS, SO IT WOULD BE ME, TOM AND WILLIAM IN ONE ROOM. WE WERE A REALLY CLOSE-KNIT FAMILY AND WHEREVER WE LIVED IT WAS ALWAYS A VERY BUSY, LOUD AND HECTIC BUT FUN HOUSE!'

'I USED TO GO ROUND TO UNCLE JOHNNY'S HOUSE ALL THE TIME, AND THERE'D ALWAYS BE A GUITAR RESTING AGAINST A CHAIR OR HANGING UP ON THE WALL. I DIDN'T START PLAYING GUITAR UNTIL SOME YEARS LATER BUT I WAS ALWAYS LISTENING TO UNCLE JOHNNY PLAY. HE'S LIKE A BIG KID HIMSELF, SO WHEN I WENT ROUND TO SEE SID WE'D BE ALLOWED TO HAVE MASSIVE COMICS AND SUPERHEROES NIGHTS.'

I used to go round to Uncle Johnny's house all the time, and there'd always be a guitar resting against a chair or hanging up on the wall. I didn't start playing guitar until some years later but I was always listening to Uncle Johnny play. He's like a big kid himself, so when I went round to see Sid we'd be allowed to have massive comics and superheroes nights, *Star Wars* and all that, just being geeks really. I've never been sporty, it was all about geeky games, sci-fi and (later) horror movies.

My mum was not so much into music as her brother. She can play guitar and even used to write songs, but we would all laugh with her when she played her stuff at family nights. Mum would be the one that would sing a song for a joke. Johnny probably gets it from my grandad, Dave 'Busker' Harris, who plays guitar, accordion, harmonica and drums. He is a genuine multi-instrumentalist. He used to gig loads but these days he mostly plays in old people's homes to all the retired folks. Music was generally always around in our family. Whenever there was a sunny day we would all go to Nan's for a barbecue, then watch a film and, after that, we'd get the instruments out and Johnny would play some songs, Mum would sing, Grandad too. Happy memories. So music was always there.

Like I said earlier, at this young age I wasn't playing music myself. There was a reason why I enjoyed sitting in my room, playing on a console with Sid. I'm not going to pretend and say I had a great time at school. I didn't. I was bullied for years. I never really stayed in one place long enough to make really good mates, plus I always seemed to move school at inconvenient times, such as when I was about to go to secondary school. I was always thrown in at the deep end and had to try to make new friends, but then we'd move again. I was always the 'new boy' and, to make matters worse, I was chubby. Not a good combination.

Consequently, I was bullied really badly. I was always getting called fatty and one kid always mocked me as Teletubby Boy. I didn't realise that you could change the way you looked; I just thought I was a fat person and that was that. When we moved to one seaside town the lifestyle there didn't help because every break and lunchtime kids would go and buy fish and chips, so I did get chubby. Perfect for the bullies.

'IT GOT TO THE POINT WHERE I USED TO RUN OUT OF SCHOOL HALFWAY THROUGH THE DAY. WE USED TO LIVE BY THE BACK GATES TO THE SCHOOL AT THE END OF THIS TINY PATH, SO I WOULD LITERALLY RUN OUT OF THE GATES, CRYING, PAST THE TEACHER.'

A lot of the time it was verbal bullying, but not exclusively – for example, one time I tried to stand up for myself and this kid headbutted me. It didn't help that I wasn't into sports. I was just this geeky, chubby new kid, who no one wanted to be friends with.

The subjects that interested me didn't help either. For example, there was no music department at one particular school. It was all about sports and no one gave a crap about anything artistic. I was always the last one to be picked for sports teams. I really tried to make friends – one lunchtime there were these two boys who were really quite geeky as well, but they were friends with each other, so I tried becoming friends with them. They told me to meet them in the playground later but when I got there they just ran away laughing, so I was left on my own. Again.

At one secondary school I was bullied very badly for over two years. I even spoke to the head teacher but no one dealt with it. Well, they did try one thing – for three days they took me out of all my lessons and put me in a room on my own to learn. They got kids in my class to bring work to me, but the people they picked were the very same kids that were bullying me!

It got to the point where I used to run out of school halfway through the day. We used to live by the back gates to the school at the end of this tiny path, so I would literally run out of the gates, crying, past the teacher. The teachers didn't do anything to stop the bullying. In fact, let's be honest here, some of them picked on me too, giving me random detentions and stuff like that. I wasn't a sporty one, so they had no interest in me. Eventually I couldn't take any more and I ended up not going to school. I refused to go in. I was frightened and I was sick of it. I had no friends, I didn't know what to do and no one at the school seemed to want to help me, so I refused to go.

I would sit at home and play games instead. I *loved* my computer games. Then when Sid came home from school he'd join me and we'd play for hours and hours. Watching my brother Will playing *The Legend of Zelda* on the Nintendo 64 is one of my best childhood memories, or waking up at silly o' clock in the morning with him to play that or *Pokémon Stadium*.

To get through those horrible times I threw myself into virtual-reality; I deliberately took myself away from life as much as I could. It got to the point where my mum was getting in trouble over my poor attendance, but there was no way I would let her take me to school, I said they could drag me in, but I would just walk back. Why would you want to go somewhere to be treated like that? That started to cause tension with Mum, because obviously she was trying her best to get me to school, so I started going round to my nan's, because she was a bit softer with me.

Away from the support at home, I also found comfort talking to my Uncle Johnny. I used to call up and tell him I was being bullied again and he would tell me to go round, see Sid and hang out at his place. When I was with Johnny I felt comfortable because I could be myself and have fun, whether it was driving to the beach at midnight with him and his girlfriend Anda and Sid, or playing video games, or listening to his guitar, whatever. It was great just to be allowed to be a kid and have a nice time.

Eventually the bullying became unbearable so I stopped going in to school altogether and did my work from home. This wasn't allowed officially, but that was the only way I was prepared to do the work. This absence from school went on for eighteen months and by the end I actually wanted to go back and try

again, because at this point we'd moved to Cheddar. I was still fat, but the new place was a design and technology school, so they had a greater focus on artistic subjects, which was really good news at last. There were classes for Art, Drama and Music too, although I didn't actually take Music as one of my subjects. I was massively into art, so I actually took two GCSEs in it! And, thankfully, I was bullied much, much less (although there was always the odd comment).

You might wonder how I got into music if I didn't even take it as a subject at school. Well, my nan used to take me to shows all the time. Whenever she could we would go and see a musical, so I knew I liked drama and, of course, I'd already been listening to my Uncle Johnny's albums and music for years. At the time he lodged with an actor and whenever I went around there I'd hear all these fantastic stories of life in that world. Then after Johnny's band came to an end, he set up this recording studio in his house and I'd go round there and watch him laying tracks down and writing material. Little by little I was being drawn into the world of singing, acting and performing and I really started to love it.

I used to be really into poppy stuff – S Club 7, S Club Juniors, Sugababes, Busted were quite cool, a bit of McFly – but then because Uncle Johnny was a rock star I also got into rock stuff like Perfect Circle, Sunna, Evanescence, Guns N' Roses, AC/DC and heavy, older rock bands. It was perhaps inevitable that I would pick up one of Johnny's guitars and start messing around, and he showed me a few basic chords and I also learnt some techniques myself from YouTube. I started to really crave my own guitar, encouraged even more by watching Grandad, Dave 'Busker' Harris, doing open-mike nights. One night I was really enjoying watching him play when my nan turned to me and said, 'Why don't you get up and play, George?' I was too nervous, so I said, 'Because I haven't got my own guitar.' She replied, 'Well, if me and your grandad got you a guitar, would you go up and play then?'

A few days later, Grandad took me to the local music shop and we spent ages picking the best guitar he could afford; he spent so much time and attention helping me. Then he really pressed the shop owner for a brilliant deal and somehow he managed to get a case thrown in and some other bits and pieces. After taking all this time setting me up we came out all excited and because we'd been so long his car had been clamped! I still didn't have the courage to do the open-mike nights, though!

The first song I learnt myself in full was 'Apologize' by One Republic, and soon after I also studied loads of other pop songs. Sid started learning guitar as well and we often played 'School of Rock' as a duet, both of us singing along. We started going to various open-mike nights around Somerset with Nan and Grandad, and my fascination with music and the guitar just kept building.

I tried hanging out with loads of different kids at Cheddar but sometimes found out that they were pretty fake, so I learnt about how people can be two-faced. I did manage to find myself a nice group of friends though, both boys and girls. They were mostly the indie kids, artistic and into drama and music like me. Like I said, that school really encouraged the artistic side in all the kids there, and it was at an audition for a production of *Animal Farm* that I had a pretty massive moment for me, in terms of getting approval from my school peers. I'd had a really small part in the previous year's version of *Much Ado About Nothing*, but *Animal Farm* was a singing adaptation. I went along to the audition just to see what it was like. I didn't even know if I was a good singer or not and I'd certainly never really sung in public before. We were in this classroom and

they played the song a few times for us to get familiar with it and then the plan was for each student to sing a few lines. I was crapping myself when it came along to me but I sang it really well and everybody was so shocked. I can still see the looks on their faces now! The teacher was more shocked than anyone else. When I'd finished my lines, everyone turned to me and clapped. I got the part as Raven and a whole load of credibility and popularity as a result. For a kid who was so used to being bullied and having no mates, that was a *big* deal.

A lot of my friends were girls around this time. One girl I fancied was in love with a close friend of mine, who was also a girl, but I didn't find out until later! I was never interested in girls initially because they were never interested in me. I had a few brief girlfriends. I went out with a girl called Daisy for a couple of months, then her best friend, then there was Anna, who was a Christian, and I used to go to church every weekend just so she would like me. But, no, never any serious girlfriends.

I actually did pretty well in my GCSEs, especially at Art, which I absolutely loved. I was constantly filling sketchbooks with ideas and drawings; I was really in my element. By now we'd moved again and I had an hour-long commute, so I'd done the last half-year studying from home, but I still got good grades. I was really pleased. I had no idea of what career I was going to follow at this point, although I'd flirted with the thought of being a barrister like my dad, but increasingly I wanted to do something with art. When it came to choosing a college, I went to all these open days and eventually chose Weston College, although mainly because they'd told me that every student got an Apple Mac!

I was at Weston College for two years and I don't mind saying I did extremely well. I got a distinction in everything, except one merit, which earned me a BTEC in Graphic Design. I loved it. My tutor Rachel was brilliant; she really inspired me to work at my graphics and we have since become great friends! Along the way I'd found out there was loads of money in graphics, so I decided to set up my own little company which I called Dreamtime Design. By now I was spending a lot of time with my other cousin Brad, who was also into graphics and computers, and he set up a company too. We got business cards made and websites set up and started going round local businesses offering our design services. I'd put together a portfolio with all my college work and people seemed to really like the idea that these young lads were having a crack at something, so we actually got quite a decent bit of freelance work.

George paul shelley

For Year One of college I was still quite chubby and baby-faced, but by the start of Year Two I'd had a growth spurt over the summer holidays and slimmed out, and a few of my girl mates said, 'Oh my God, look at George!', which was nice for me to hear. People at college were treating me nicely, the teachers were encouraging me to be artistic in all sorts of ways, and it was a good period in my life. I became much more outgoing and would always be messing about, trying to make people laugh. That annoyed a few people because I would still do well with my grades. I worked best in my bedroom, which was downstairs next to the kitchen. It felt like my own apartment. My desk was huge, I had my laptop, my TV, my games – it was my own little snug bubble, so I'd shut the door and get all my work done to the best of my ability, then I'd go in to college on deadline day, hand it in and get a distinction. Some people found that frustrating and let me know that, but generally it was really enjoyable being reasonably popular for probably the first time in my entire school life.

I was heavily into my guitar playing by now and if there was a party I would inevitably end up bringing it out and playing a few tunes. I still wasn't performing at the open-mike nights but I had started writing my own songs. When I was in college my brother was in the Marines so I wrote a song about his life in the army. It was really cheesy. It was called 'Brotherhood' and the lyrics were about our own brotherhood but also the army brotherhood! Like I said, cheesy! My Uncle Johnny got me in his studio to record this song and then my mum somehow gave it to someone 'important' and they said it might be used as a charity single. I remember when Mum told me that I was hyperventilating I was so excited, but nothing actually came of it because when we were supposed to go and meet the people who were interested I was too self-conscious about the song to go. So it was my fault really.

I was still massively into gaming and because of my graphics background, I'd started thinking maybe I could design web pages for gaming 'zines, or covers for games themselves, or perhaps even set up my own reviews website. If I am being completely honest, at this point gaming was still a higher priority for me than music (that would change!). This was partly because my family were worried that music wasn't a very secure career. Also, I was still very self-conscious about how I looked, probably a hangover from my chubby days. Although now I was worried because I looked really young and some people used to take the mickey out of me for that. I didn't start driving lessons like a lot of my mates because of looking so young. I just felt awkward about it, and I still don't drive yet. I guess I didn't grow up mentally because I wasn't growing up physically. Any spare time I had I would chill out or just play games, usually fuelled by daft amounts of coffee, which I was addicted to. I didn't think about having girlfriends at all, it was just me and Brad chilling out.

I really came out of myself during college, though. I had friends and I was doing well in class, so I was like a different person: hyper, buzzing, talking really fast and loud and being the centre of attention all the time, which is weird because three years before I was this timid little fat kid. One day I was messing about on the bus to college, telling everyone really loudly about this story when my brother had meningitis and had had to have this massive needle in his bum, and people were laughing and joking along. A few days later I was at a house party when this girl drunkenly tripped down some stairs and laughed as she stood up, then looked at me and went, 'You're meningitis boy!' That was Emily, my crazy, mad best friend, and we've been pretty much inseparable since.

We did – and still do – everything together, and perhaps under-standably her boyfriend at the time was quite jealous because she would spend every spare minute with me. But we've never dated; we're just mates. She once said she'd fancied me a bit at first, but that she 'soon got over it'. Thanks, Emily!

I spent all my free time with Emily, Brad or my nan. By this point my Uncle Johnny lived in a cabin in the woods and had a studio up there, so I was still regularly experimenting with writing my own material. I started doing a degree course in graphic design at the same college because I felt happy there and I also got a job in Starbucks, which was where I met my first serious girlfriend, a girl called Bec, who was my supervisor. The travelling to my university course proved too much, so in the end I rented a flat with my brother Will just round the corner from the college in Weston-super-Mare. It was a nice flat by the seaside, with this cool little balcony. That was a really enjoyable period because I felt self-reliant for the first time in my life. I had money coming in from my part-time jobs (I'd moved to work in Costa by now!), I had my friends over all the time, and I could do whatever I wanted whenever I wanted. It was brilliant. Actually, Will wasn't there much because he was away with the Marines so often, which meant that most of the time I was either there on my own playing on my guitar or Emily would be round.

While I was at that flat I watched *X Factor* and it was Little Mix's year, 2011. I used to watch bits and bobs from the show – I was really into it the year Jedward were on, Leona Lewis too – but it was never a massive thing for me, partly because I never really sang at that point in my life. Even as late as 2011 I was pretty cut off from the music industry, to be honest, although by then I was pretty obsessed with playing my guitar all the time.

In that series Little Mix were my favourites. I really wanted them to win. My brother, his girlfriend and Emily and me used to sit down and watch the show every Saturday and Sunday night religiously. We all got into it massively, and when Little Mix won I was over the moon. As the weeks had gone by we'd discussed what it would be like to go on the show, but I never really considered it seriously because I thought it was mainly for power singers, people like Leona, and I wasn't confident enough in my voice at that point. I knew I had an interesting tone, but I didn't feel I had the range that some of those *X Factor* winners boasted. One weekend I asked Emily for her honest opinion, 'What do you reckon would happen if I entered?' She said, 'Well, you've got the image!' We laughed and then she said, 'I'm not sure you would get through as a solo singer. Maybe go back in a couple more years when your voice has developed? Maybe they will put you in a group?' That sounded like fair advice but at that point it was all about my guitar so I didn't really fancy that.

Then after one show late in the 2011 series, Emily and my brother had left the room and I was just sitting there on my own with the *X Factor* closing credits. Then that big booming voice came on the TV and said, 'You can apply for *X Factor* now!' I know this sounds daft but it felt really weird, like he was talking directly to me. It was such an odd feeling. It was almost like the TV was telling me to do it; I was transfixed by his voice and what he was saying.

'THEN THAT BIG BOOMING VOICE CAME ON THE TV AND SAID, 'YOU CAN APPLY FOR **X FACTOR** NOW!' I KNOW THIS SOUNDS DAFT BUT IT FELT REALLY WEIRD, LIKE HE WAS TALKING DIRECTLY TO ME. IT WAS SUCH AN ODD FEELING. IT WAS ALMOST LIKE THE TV WAS TELLING ME TO DO IT.'

Over the next few weeks I couldn't get that voice out of my head. It was swirling round and round in my brain: 'Apply now!'

I learnt more new songs after Christmas, most notably 'Toxic' by Britney Spears and 'Grenade' by Bruno Mars, plus my range had improved a lot. My voice had dropped and I had more power too, so my projection was far better and my tone seemed richer. I was gaining confidence in my voice all the time. One time round my grandad's, Dave 'Busker' Harris even said to me, 'You should go on that *X Factor* malarkey!'

Over the next few months, that idea still kept swimming around in my head as I was doing my uni projects, working at Costa and hanging out at the flat. In May it was time to go camping – every year since I was born my family has gone camping to this place in Cornwall over the Whitsun week, and because lots of other families go there each year too we have made some close friends (such as Abi and Aaron, who are still a massive part of my life). In May 2012 I went and – of course – I took my guitar. One night I was playing a few tunes to some girls who I'd made friends with and they kept saying, 'You should go on *X Factor*.' That thought again.

'APPLY NOW!'

THEN ONE NIGHT I WAS ON MY LAPTOP AND A BANNER ADVERT POPPED UP SAYING, 'APPLY FOR X FACTOR'. ONE OF THE AUDITIONS WAS AT CARDIFF SO I FILLED IN THE FORM AND THOUGHT NOTHING MORE OF IT. WEEKS WENT BY AND I'D FORGOTTEN ABOUT EVEN FILLING IT IN, BECAUSE I WAS SO BUSY WITH UNI WORK, GAMING AND PLAYING MY GUITAR. THEN I LOGGED ON TO MY COMPUTER ONE AFTERNOON AND THERE WAS AN EMAIL FROM THE X FACTOR SAYING I HAD BEEN ACCEPTED ON TO THE SHOW AND THAT I HAD AN AUDITION IN CARDIFF AT THE END OF THE MONTH. I HAD THREE WEEKS TO PREPARE FOR AN AFTERNOON THAT WOULD CHANGE MY LIFE.

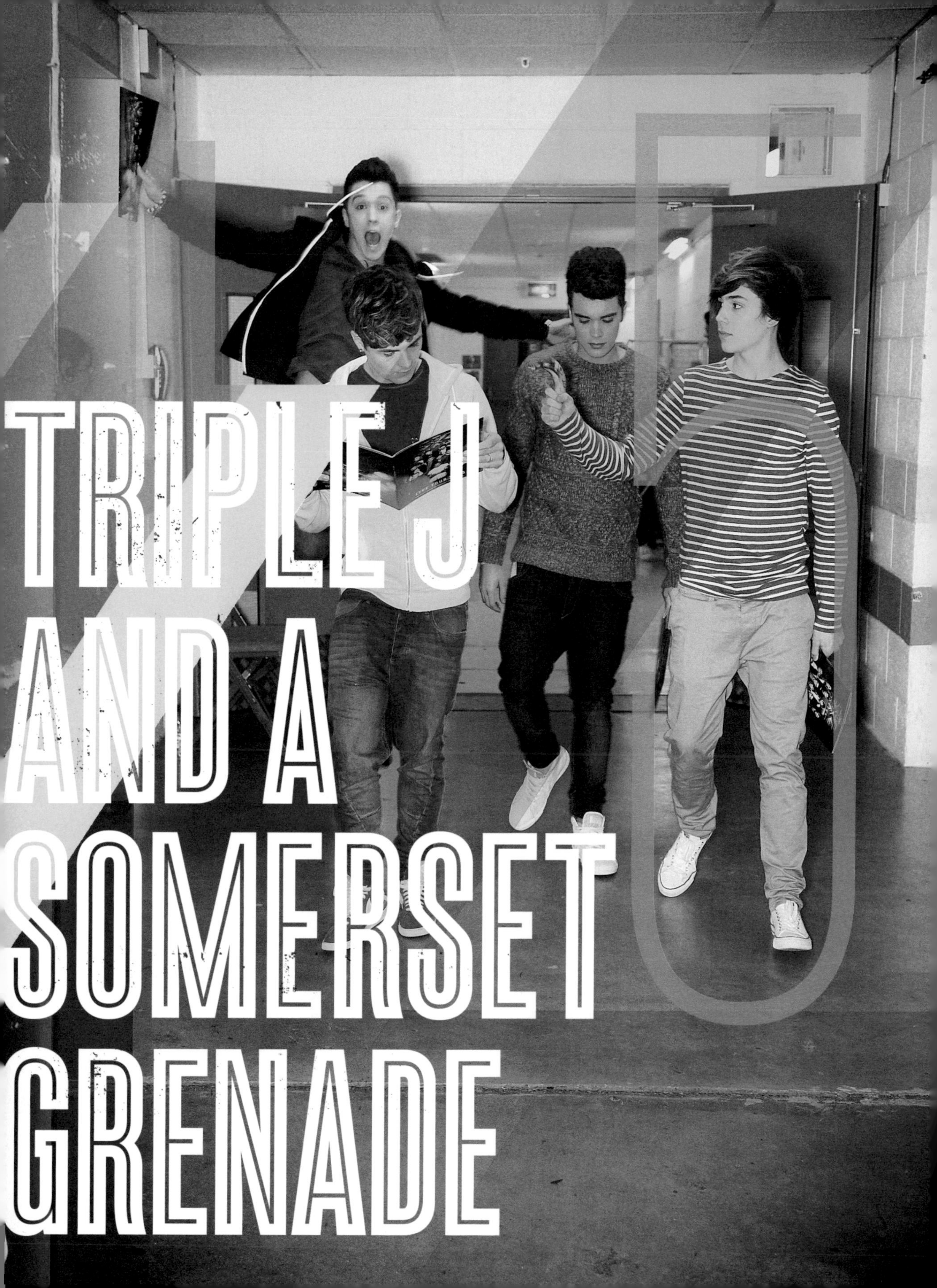

TRIPLE J
AND A
SOMERSET
GRENADE

JAYMI: It was hard for me to keep going back to *X Factor* each year, especially after five years of nothing working out for me. I thought about setting up my own boy band for the 2012 series of the show but nothing came of that. It is so hard to make it in a boy band; there are so many talented, good-looking people out there gunning for it. However, I was sold on being in a boy band. That is what I wanted. Then I was approached about this audition for a new boy band, a five-piece. So we started trying out various boys for the band and that's when I first met Josh.

JOSH: Remember, I'd only gone to the audition because the bloody window cleaner had woken me up! Well, I reluctantly drove down to Brighton, walked in the room and all the time I was thinking, *What am I doing here? Why am I doing this again?* I wasn't sure I could bring myself to get to know another group of boys only to get my heart broken again by the band not working out. I don't mind admitting, I was scared. But then I was introduced to Jaymi and he was something altogether different. Very different.

JAYMI: When I first met Josh, I thought, *God, this boy can sing. This boy is so talented . . .* It obviously helped that he was lovely-looking too, but I just felt a connection with him. There was a chemistry, wasn't there?

JOSH: Definitely! The other lads in the room were cool and everything, but I was drawn to Jaymi. I'd heard about his years of experience and that was mightily impressive, and then I heard him sing! Wow! I just started to get this positive feeling inside, pushing all the negative thoughts to one side. *This could work . . .*

JAYMI: I remember thinking, *He is amazing, great tone, lovely-looking. We could do this.* It wasn't for a while that we realised our paths had actually crossed before. The penny dropped that we had both gone to Sylvia Young's at the same time.

JOSH: At Sylvia Young's Jaymi was the guy that I used to really look up to and think, *Oh my God, he's so talented.* He used to help out the younger kids all the time; he was so generous with his advice and time. He actually used to say to me, 'You should try out for *X Factor*, Josh!' I just thought he had the best voice in the world.

'**JOSH:** REMEMBER, I'D ONLY GONE TO THE AUDITION BECAUSE THE BLOODY WINDOW CLEANER HAD WOKEN ME UP! WELL, I RELUCTANTLY DROVE DOWN TO BRIGHTON, WALKED IN THE ROOM AND ALL THE TIME I WAS THINKING, **WHAT AM I DOING HERE? WHY AM I DOING THIS AGAIN?** I WASN'T SURE I COULD BRING MYSELF TO GET TO KNOW ANOTHER GROUP OF BOYS ONLY TO GET MY HEART BROKEN AGAIN BY THE BAND NOT WORKING OUT. I DON'T MIND ADMITTING, I WAS SCARED.'

JAYMI: The memories came back from Sylvia Young's and I remembered Josh being really good even way back then. So I knew he was going to be right for this new band. One hundred per cent. But we still needed another boy. That's where JJ came in.

JJ: I'd had that email while I was on holiday in Turkey and so when I got back I had headed down to the audition too. I was nervous when I first walked into that room to meet Jaymi, Josh and the other lads, I don't mind admitting. Josh and Jaymi were really nice to me straight away and tried their best to make me feel comfortable and at ease. However, I sat there listening to them tell me about their experience – Jaymi's done the *X Factor* four times, he's this incredible singer, toured with Westlife and all that, and Josh is an amazing singer too, he's been in all these boy-band projects previously, toured with Boyzone. I was only used to singing in front of, like, fifty people. So I was naturally worrying and thinking, *Am I good enough for these boys?*

JAYMI: JJ, you were brilliant straight away! There was something about him that was hilarious, and I just knew that this kid was gonna be right for us. Yes, he was desperate to do it, but I knew that meant he wanted success as much as me. I knew JJ was special. He made us laugh, he had a good voice, he was also lovely-looking and had this great personality, really infectious.

JOSH: JJ was very quiet at first but he gradually came out of his shell and felt more comfortable. Over the next few months, though, not much actually happened with the new band. There was me, Jaymi and JJ, plus these other two lads, but actually we did very little. I think we only met up about four times and there were certainly no gigs or tours or anything concrete like that.

JJ: Literally nothing happened. Nothing came of it. People at home were like, 'Oh, you are in a band. Great!' But nothing was happening. We got together in November 2011, but by April 2012 I must have seen them about four times. That's what it was like. It wasn't a band really.

JOSH: We were rehearsing occasionally and what that did for me was highlight how well me, Jaymi and JJ sounded together, but less so the other two lads. I don't know what it was, but when I was singing with Jaymi and JJ I got a really good vibe, something felt different. I felt so positive towards Jaymi and JJ's vocals. There seemed to be an instant chemistry, vocally and with our personalities, but that wasn't there with the other two lads (speaking for myself anyway). Whenever we practised as a five-piece I felt something was not right, whereas us three blended well. It just didn't work as a five-piece.

By this stage, all the talk of what might happen with this boy band just went in one ear and out the other for me. I took everything with a pinch of salt, so I still worked every day in IT, that was my Plan B, my fall-back. We weren't gigging at all, then we started falling out with each other when we did all meet up. It just fell apart.

Then one day I was in my car and JJ rang, so I pulled over and he said, 'I really want to do *X Factor*, Josh.' I said, 'So do I, JJ, so do I.' So we rang Jaymi and suggested the same and that's how Triple J came about.

JAYMI: It was actually rather awkward for me in this set-up – we were called Brooklyn – because one of the other two lads was one of my very best friends, Billy. The problem was that I knew it wasn't working as a five-piece. It got to the point where me, Josh and JJ were chatting about starting a three-piece, but that was difficult for me because it felt like the right thing to do but I had to consider Billy too. It was a hard decision to choose between Billy or the band, but at that point I was so tired of not making it, I was like, *I am always being nice but that just seems to cost me.* You know, nice guys finish last and all that. My mum sat me down and said I had to stop worrying about everyone else. So I made my decision to leave that band and I explained this to Billy and he did understand. He was upset but he understood. He is still a great friend.

JJ: We had realised that there weren't any three-piece boy bands out there, and we thought that was a gap in the market. So we decided to form a three-piece group, literally about three days before the *X Factor*! If I remember rightly, this was on a Friday night and the auditions were on the Tuesday! So over the weekend we got together in Jaymi's living room in Luton and rehearsed for hours, trying out various songs. We hadn't got a clue about styling, we were trying on all these outfits and also there were no three-part harmonies, it was all pretty fly-by-the-seat-of-your-pants stuff. Remember we'd not even done a gig together as a five-piece . . .

JOSH: Looking back it was nuts, wasn't it? Ha ha! But there was something between the three of us that felt right. I know people overuse the word 'chemistry', but there was definitely something there. But we weren't ready, were we?

JJ: We literally were not ready! We should have had longer to prepare, but we didn't, so it was a case of just getting on with it. We thought, *Let's just try and see what happens.* Jaymi lived in Luton, Josh lived in Windsor and I was in Cambridge, so it wasn't exactly convenient for getting to see each other but we did as much as we could, driving for hours and hours in those few short days, getting ourselves into gear.

JAYMI: We didn't even have a band name until the very last second, when we finally came up with Triple J because of our first names. I know it's easy to say now, but after all those years of struggling and being rejected, I honestly had such a good feeling, something was telling me this was the year. I was fighting for it, and I knew Josh and JJ were fighting for it as well, so I felt like I had someone in my corner. So off we went to the *X Factor* first-stage auditions. It was time to see what Triple J were made of.

JJ: At those preliminary auditions I felt fine and quite relaxed all day leading up to our slot, but as soon as we were called up I found it very intimidating. You go into this room and there's either one or two people just sitting there looking at you, no big production, just your voices and them. It's pretty daunting. Luckily I had Jaymi and Josh with me to calm my nerves and it was great to know that they had been through these early stages before.

JAYMI: We felt good at the first-stage auditions, and even though we had not had much time we sang well. The experience that me and Josh had of previous shows meant we took this in our stride quite well, but getting through was just a small start. It was all about what the judges would think when we got to the televised auditions.

'**JOSH:** THEN ONE DAY I WAS IN MY CAR AND JJ RANG, SO I PULLED OVER AND HE SAID, "I REALLY WANT TO DO **X FACTOR**, JOSH." I SAID, "SO DO I, JJ, SO DO I." SO WE RANG JAYMI AND SUGGESTED THE SAME AND THAT'S HOW **TRIPLE J** CAME ABOUT.'

GEORGE: Of course, I was oblivious to all this because I hadn't yet met the boys. I was down in Bristol still reeling from the fact *X Factor* wanted me to audition as a soloist. As soon as I got the email from *X Factor* I started panicking. I just thought I hadn't got a chance. I was imagining how many talented people would be there with guitars. Emily tried to calm my nerves and helped me choose my songs. She said, 'Trust me, have faith. I've got a really weird feeling about this.' I even got myself a singing teacher for the month to get totally ready. But I was still panicking and at one point I said to Grandad, 'I've decided I am not going,' and he said, 'George, if you don't go, you will regret it for the rest of your life. You have to go.'

Before you get through to sing in front of the famous judges, you have to do the two first-stage auditions that the boys have just mentioned. Of course, Josh and Jaymi knew all about this, so they pretty much sailed through this stage, but for me it was a really big deal. Huge, in fact. On the day before these opening auditions I got the train to Cardiff with Emily, Brad and his little sister, Bron, and we stayed in a Premier Inn family room. I didn't sleep a wink, then got up at 5 a.m. and we were in the queue at 6 a.m., but there were already a few hundred people in front of me. By 8 a.m. there were thousands of people in the queue and that's when it really dawned on me how massive the competition was going to be. Remember, at this point I had never even gigged in front of anyone, apart from a few open-mike nights when I was much younger and at the odd teenage party or camp-site barbecue.

When my name was called, I went into a booth and there was this man sitting there with dark sunglasses on. It took me ages to start singing. I was crapping myself, and somehow I managed to perform 'Grenade' in the wrong key! I was singing and thinking, *This is not high enough!* There's a really long note in that song and I remember looking up at the sun and nearly fainting and toppling over. My mouth was dry and my heart was beating, it was the most nerve-wracking thing I'd ever done at that point. The man said I had a nice tone but asked me if I knew another song in a higher key. Off the top of my head I just suggested Britney Spears's 'Toxic'. I sang the chorus a cappella and it was hard. I was so close to him and I could hear other people around me singing in similar booths. But he said, 'I like your tone. I like you. You are through. See you tomorrow!'

I was so excited I could have exploded. I ran out to Emily, Brad and Bron and we all went crazy. So it was back to the Premier Inn, we had some tea at Wagamama and we were all buzzing. Weirdest feeling ever. At this stage I knew nothing was being filmed for TV yet, so I didn't mind if it went wrong the next day because no one would ever know, so it wouldn't be embarrassing.

We stayed up really late, but then we all slept through our alarms the next day! I was horrified when I woke up. The clock said 7 a.m. and I was supposed to be at the auditions at 7.15 a.m. Luckily I'd met a lad called Abdul the previous day and followed him on Twitter, so I tweeted him and said, 'I need help!' He said they were still queuing to get in but that I had to be quick. This is no word of a lie: when I ran up to the desk the lady was literally just standing up to leave and close the auditions off. I'd made it by the skin of my teeth.

This time there were two people sat behind a desk, but first there was loads more waiting around while trying to control my nerves. They sent me in and said, 'Stand on the X, please,' but I was so nervous and relieved to have not missed the audition that I started babbling about being late and oversleeping at the Premier Inn and all that. They found that really funny and seemed to warm to me, so I sang 'Toxic' again. They didn't try to hide the fact they were enjoying it. So I got put through to yet another preliminary audition, this time in front of a camera. I sang with my guitar first, then they asked me to sing without it too, so I did 'Grenade'. It had all been going so well, but after this final audition they just politely said, 'Thanks, George. We have your footage. We will be in touch. Bye.'

I had to go back home, back to uni, and I don't mind saying I was gutted. I'd had the buzz of getting through, but I hadn't actually got anywhere really. If they said 'No' now it would have been devastating after all that initial excitement. For several weeks I heard nothing and I started to lose concentration at uni. I was kind of coasting really, messing about, playing games too much and stuff like that. I felt like I was at a standstill.

This might sound a bit odd, but over the years if me and Mum were ever feeling crap or bored, we would decorate a bedroom, so one afternoon during this frustrating period we went down to B&Q to distract ourselves and make my bedroom nice. On the way back in the car my phone went and it was a blocked number. *Do I answer it?* I thought.

I PICKED UP THE PHONE.
IT WAS A RESEARCHER FROM X FACTOR.

'HI, GEORGE.
I'M PHONING ABOUT YOUR
AUDITION. I'M PLEASED TO
TELL YOU THAT YOU HAVE
BEEN CHOSEN TO SING ON
TV IN FRONT OF THE JUDGES!'

I COULDN'T BELIEVE IT!

I STARTED KICKING THE DASHBOARD WITH EXCITEMENT
AND MUM SPED HOME SO WE COULD CELEBRATE . . .
IT WAS JUST ONE OF THE BEST FEELINGS EVER.

X FACTOR, OUR FIRST

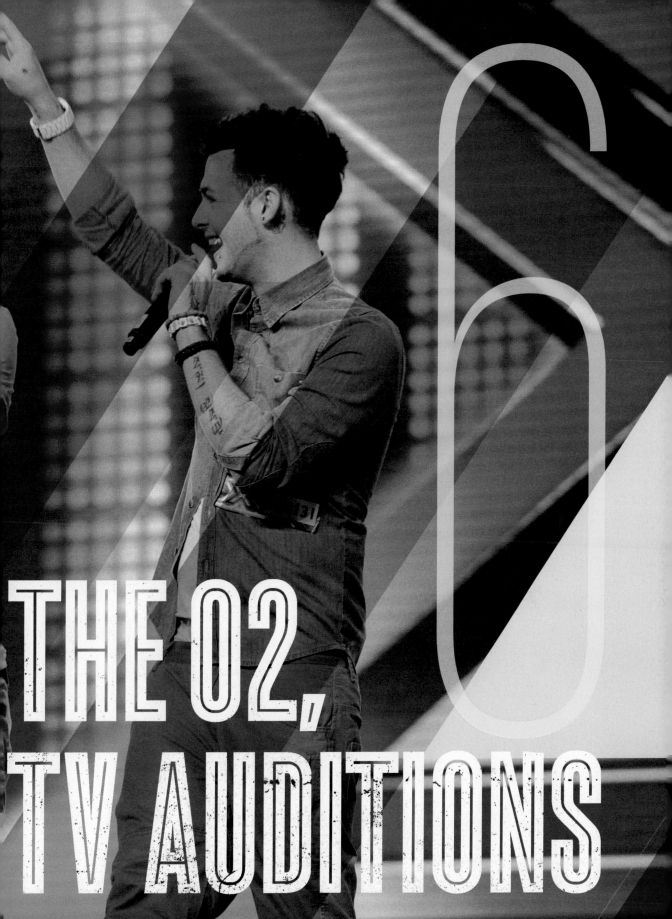

THE 02,
TV AUDITIONS

JAYMI: When we got to the O2 for the *X Factor* live TV audition in front of the judges I was so determined, so focused. I was *definitely* getting to live shows this year.

JJ: That's the difference between me and you at that point, Jaymi! I was really nervous because I just kept thinking, *Will the judges look at me and say I'm not as experienced as the other two? And say I wasn't good enough to be singing with them . . .*

JOSH: Ha ha! You shouldn't have been worrying like that, JJ! I'd done *X Factor* before, as you all know, but I was still nervous. This was my last chance, remember? The stakes were really high for me. On the other hand, because we had been together for such a ridiculously short period of time, I didn't actually expect to get through. That just seemed against the odds. I thought maybe we had a chance to get to bootcamp, but after that? No chance. I wasn't being negative. I think I was just being realistic after failing so many times. And there was an element of fear too, because I knew if this didn't work, then that really was the end of me and singing.

JJ: I was like, *We are going to sing at the O2. Wicked! I can't believe it!* We had this little thing where we had tied our hoods up tightly round our faces – you can just see it on the YouTube clip. I guess we were trying to find some sort of band identity. Before the audition we had been working really hard on Twitter, asking people to follow us, saying Triple J was going to be the next big boy band, but I think we only had a few hundred followers before we went on TV.

JAYMI: Our families had come along with us and we were all congregating backstage waiting for our turn. You have to remember that at this point we had never performed in public before as Triple J. Literally our first ever performance was in front of 10,000 people and those four judges: Gary Barlow, Rita Ora, Tulisa and Louis Walsh. It's crazy, really, looking back.

JJ: My family has had nothing to do with music before me, and no one has ever been involved in music professionally, so for them it was a proud moment. I remember I was fine all day, then at about 3 p.m. they said, 'Triple J, you are up next!' and at that point I went, 'Crap!' I know Josh and Jaymi were more relaxed because they had been there before but it was massive for me. I'd never really sung in front of anyone, literally just karaoke, and even then I only used to look at the screen. Now I was about to sing in front of thousands of people. I could hear the crowd, it was deafening, and I could hear the judges' comments for other contestants, and it was all making me really nervous. Then I looked over at my mum and she was crying and I had to concentrate to not start crying myself. But then I noticed Josh was starting to get a bit nervous too! Jaymi wasn't, though. He was so in the zone, totally focused.

JAYMI: Ha ha! It might have looked like that but I can tell you I was dying inside. Absolutely dying inside. I had to cover it up, but I was so nervous.

JOSH: I was nervous too, for sure. I kept thinking, *This is on TV so it has to be the best*. Finally I had a chance to show all those people back home who doubted me that I could do this and I could sing. Plus, I thought that was quite an intimidating judging panel. We were a boy band and out there was Gary Barlow. You know, this is serious now! Funnily enough, Gary is my mum's absolute idol. She is just in love with him and before we went on she said to me, 'Try your best, Josh, and even if you don't get through, can you just try to get me Gary's autograph?' Thanks, Mum!

JJ: The people on just before us were booed. I was thinking, *Oh my God, what have I got myself into?* I am quite laidback. I don't think about things until the last minute usually. So when I heard the boos of the crowd I thought, *Okay, this is serious*. They called us out and we walked on to the stage in front of all those people, for our first ever public performance as Triple J. We sang Rihanna's 'We Found Love', which was potentially a bad song choice because a lot of people had been singing it that day so we were worried the audience and judges might be sick of it. However, we had given it a twist with an acoustic backing track, which we thought sounded really cool. It was different so we thought we would give it a try. As it turned out, we needn't have been concerned.

JOSH: We felt that as a boy band it was Gary and Louis that we needed to make the biggest first impression on. Gary was smiling during the audition so as I sang I sensed it was going well, and the crowd seemed to be really getting into it as well.

JJ: Halfway through the song Jaymi was supposed to do this massive ad-lib, but they stopped us! Gary Barlow put his hand up, so now we were panicking . . . had we done enough?

JAYMI: COME ON, JJ, WE SMASHED IT! I'M NOT GONNA PRETEND AND SAY OTHERWISE. WE REALLY NAILED IT. I'M SO PROUD OF THAT PERFORMANCE. IF YOU THINK ABOUT THE TIME WE HAD TO PREPARE, OUR LEAD-UP TO THE AUDITION, THERE WAS SO MUCH PRESSURE AND THE ODDS WERE AGAINST US.

TULISA SAID,

'THIS IS WHAT BOY BANDS ARE ABOUT, GOOD-LOOKING LADS . . .'

AND GUEST JUDGE RITA ORA CHIPPED IN TOO, SAYING,

'I THINK THE GIRLS WILL LOVE YOU.'

THEN CAME THE BIGGEST COMMENT WHEN GARY SAID,

'A GOOD BOY BAND IS NOT ALL ABOUT LOOKING GOOD, YOU'VE GOTTA SOUND GREAT TOO, AND YOU REALLY DO SOUND GREAT.

FOUR YESES. WELL DONE!"

JJ: We never expected such an amazing reaction as that! I ran off stage and picked up my little sister. She was crying her eyes out. She was only six and, apparently, while she was backstage she was crying that much that she kind of half passed out! We were all cheering and hugging. It was absolutely unreal. It was amazing to see my family so involved. The drive home that night back from London was amazing, the very same journey I'd made so many times after getting rejection after rejection. But not this time.

JOSH: I came running off the stage and did my football cheer, 'Yes!', with my arms punching the air like I'd scored a goal! Sharing that feeling with two other guys rather than on my own as a soloist was an amazing feeling. My stepdad hugged me and said, 'This is your year!' My mum was in tears and we were all so excited. We went to Pizza Hut that night to celebrate. And yes, I did get Gary's autograph for Mum.

JAYMI: I loved that day! That was sick. The feedback was amazing. I was really shocked, genuinely. You don't hear ones like that all the time and I was like, *That's us they are talking about!* That first audition made me realise why I do what I do and it made me want it more than ever. That night I went out with my family and celebrated. It was such a good day.

Not to sound arrogant or anything but we sailed through. Yes, we were so nervous before, but as soon as we got on stage something just happened. The song was amazing, the crowd were into us, something just switched in us. It was an incredible feeling. I had a different feeling from all the other years that I'd auditioned. I just felt like this was the start of something . . .

Watching that clip back is such an exciting experience, all those amazing memories come rushing back, all that adrenalin. One thing I will say, though (apart from the fact that we all look older), is that it looks odd watching that clip back and seeing us up there without George. I don't like that. It's not right . . .

GEORGE: At this point I still hadn't bumped into Triple J or met the boys; I was still going through this whole *X Factor* process as a soloist. I'd had about two weeks to prepare for the judges' audition and in that time I practised so hard. The night before the TV audition we stayed in the exact same Premier Inn as before and then all piled round to the side of the stage to wait for my turn.

Before you go on stage, they do all this random filming and they were chatting to Grandad about me, because I'd said what an inspiration he was to me, but the really funny thing was that he kept telling them all this random stuff and in the end they couldn't use any of the footage!

Just before I went on, another young solo boy sang and he got through, and I was convinced that he was better than me. When it comes to your turn to go on stage it is the weirdest feeling ever; just before you walk on you have to speak to Dermot for a quick interview, which is the first time you've ever met him. I introduced him to my family, which was a weird moment in itself. They tell you to act naturally while they film you preparing, but I just stood there staring at this wall!

I went up the steps and stood behind a black curtain, listening to the person before me sing, and this girl was incredible. I couldn't see her but she got four yeses. Then they called me up and as I walked out on the stage it felt so massive. I felt completely lost out there. I looked out and there were all these people staring at me, and the judges were looking at me, with Nicole sort of nodding her head. It was just the weirdest sensation ever.

I got a little cheer when I walked on, which helped ease my nerves a little bit, but then it came to my performance of 'Toxic'. It went quite well but in the chorus I sang, 'royd' instead of 'ride' in a really Bristolian accent (it's really funny because lots of Union J fans say that now!). I was dreadfully nervous. I usually smile when I sing but I didn't that day.

I know this is going to sound strange, but it felt like I was singing in slow motion. Everyone is staring at you and you're looking at the judges, trying to work out what they are thinking. If the song is going on too long they stop you and that's exactly what Gary Barlow did, which I thought could only be a bad sign.

Initially the judges said they weren't sure if I could work as a solo artist, so I sang 'Price Tag' mashed up with 'Where Is the Love?' for them too. After that, Louis said, 'You've got a great image and a good vocal.' And I got enough yeses – including Tulisa who said it was 'A massive yes!' – to put me through to bootcamp!

I was over the moon, and absolutely shocked. I genuinely didn't think I'd get through. If you watch the clip on YouTube, you can see how shocked I am because I just wander off stage completely blank-faced and walk straight past my mum to hug my little cousin Bron because she is crying so much. Then Dermot asked me loads of questions but I barely heard what he was saying and I certainly didn't answer them properly.

Obviously I was totally elated, but I was *so exhausted*. I was completely drained, and it was all a bit surreal. Once the shock had worn off, I couldn't believe it. When I got home I dropped out of university; I'd decided that singing was my total focus now. Before that TV audition I had twenty followers on Twitter. Within a day of that audition later being broadcast I had over 8,000. Something amazing was happening . . .

'I GOT A LITTLE CHEER WHEN I WALKED ON, WHICH HELPED EASE MY NERVES A LITTLE BIT, BUT THEN IT CAME TO MY PERFORMANCE OF 'TOXIC'. IT WENT QUITE WELL BUT IN THE CHORUS I SANG, "ROYD" INSTEAD OF "RIDE" IN A REALLY BRISTOLIAN ACCENT (IT'S REALLY FUNNY BECAUSE LOTS OF UNION J FANS SAY THAT NOW!). I WAS DREADFULLY NERVOUS. I USUALLY SMILE WHEN I SING BUT I DIDN'T THAT DAY.'

BOOTCAMP

JAYMI: There is about a two-month gap after the live audition until the start of bootcamp. You're allowed to tell your family you are through, so it was all very exciting, but you obviously can't tell anyone else. Knowing how little time we had to rehearse previously, we weren't about to not take full advantage of that two months so we rehearsed like dogs! It was either in my house or Josh's but we were singing constantly for those eight weeks. We were going to be so ready.

JOSH: I should point out here that I actually went on holiday for two weeks, though! That sounds slack but it was for the weirdest reason. I went because my mum and stepdad said to me, 'You should go on holiday before this, because afterwards you won't be able to go away again.' At first I was a bit like, 'What are you talking about?' They were very optimistic, like they knew what was about to happen almost. I wasn't so positive; I thought we might get to the live shows perhaps, hopefully at least to Judges' Houses, but I took their advice and went to Rhodes for a fortnight. So I turned up to bootcamp looking like an orange tomato.

JJ: Lucky you! I went back to working with the horses! Mind you, I love that so it was no hardship. Straight after the live audition I was back at the stables, earning some money, and just being excited about what bootcamp held in store for Triple J.

JOSH: We mainly spent the time getting to know each other. I had to go back to full-time IT sales, because although we were all really excited there were no guarantees, so I couldn't afford to leave my job. It was back to reality. I found it an anxious six weeks when I got back from holiday. It could be the start of the rest of my life or it could be the end of an era.

I'd say I am a massive worrier. I worry because I get scared about what might happen. And from my painful experiences in the past I knew that if things don't go well I tend to get quite depressed. That sounds a bit extreme but it takes me a while to get back to my normal self. But I can't deny that I was also very excited. I had plenty of fight left in me.

GEORGE: Bootcamp was when I first met the boys. I went there on my own obviously. Before bootcamp I sold most of my games consoles and my piano, just to get money to buy decent clothes so I would look right. So I went up to Liverpool and you all meet up in this big room, where you see everyone for the first time. It was covered in old-school wood panelling and lit by these great big chandeliers. It was such a nervous room to be in because as it filled up you started to sense the amount of competition; it was daunting to see how many people had got through. There were cameras everywhere but I was never really into competing for screen time. There were people being really fake and dancing and playing up to get on camera, but I was always in the corner just being myself. I didn't really speak to many people.

Then JLS came in and I was really star-struck. It all seemed very exciting, but then suddenly they announced that they would be sending home about ninety acts without them having had the chance to sing again. I was gutted to hear that. To go home so quickly without having had the opportunity to perform again would be awful.

JAYMI: I remember bootcamp as not being as stressful as the year before. That year had nearly killed me, honestly! For 2012 maybe I was ready for it and knew what to expect. But there's no denying it's tough . . . very long hours. They don't call it bootcamp because it's a holiday! Emotions were high and we were thinking this was a really strong year. There were some amazing characters: Rylan, Lucy Spraggan, Kye, Jahméne, James, Ella . . . Big voices, big personalities.

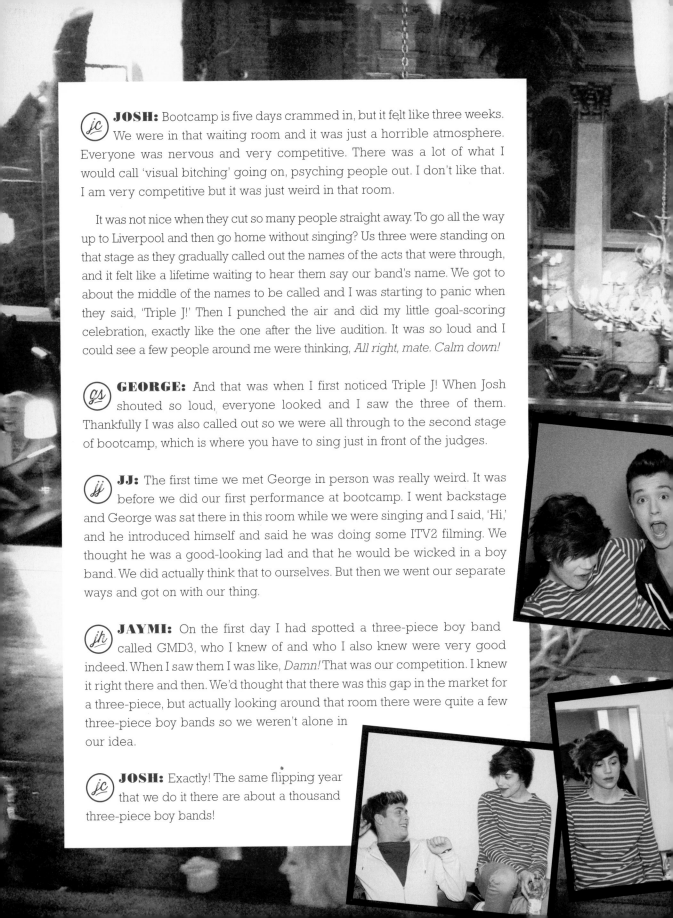

JOSH: Bootcamp is five days crammed in, but it felt like three weeks. We were in that waiting room and it was just a horrible atmosphere. Everyone was nervous and very competitive. There was a lot of what I would call 'visual bitching' going on, psyching people out. I don't like that. I am very competitive but it was just weird in that room.

It was not nice when they cut so many people straight away. To go all the way up to Liverpool and then go home without singing? Us three were standing on that stage as they gradually called out the names of the acts that were through, and it felt like a lifetime waiting to hear them say our band's name. We got to about the middle of the names to be called and I was starting to panic when they said, 'Triple J!' Then I punched the air and did my little goal-scoring celebration, exactly like the one after the live audition. It was so loud and I could see a few people around me were thinking, *All right, mate. Calm down!*

GEORGE: And that was when I first noticed Triple J! When Josh shouted so loud, everyone looked and I saw the three of them. Thankfully I was also called out so we were all through to the second stage of bootcamp, which is where you have to sing just in front of the judges.

JJ: The first time we met George in person was really weird. It was before we did our first performance at bootcamp. I went backstage and George was sat there in this room while we were singing and I said, 'Hi,' and he introduced himself and said he was doing some ITV2 filming. We thought he was a good-looking lad and that he would be wicked in a boy band. We did actually think that to ourselves. But then we went our separate ways and got on with our thing.

JAYMI: On the first day I had spotted a three-piece boy band called GMD3, who I knew of and who I also knew were very good indeed. When I saw them I was like, *Damn!* That was our competition. I knew it right there and then. We'd thought that there was this gap in the market for a three-piece, but actually looking around that room there were quite a few three-piece boy bands so we weren't alone in our idea.

JOSH: Exactly! The same flipping year that we do it there are about a thousand three-piece boy bands!

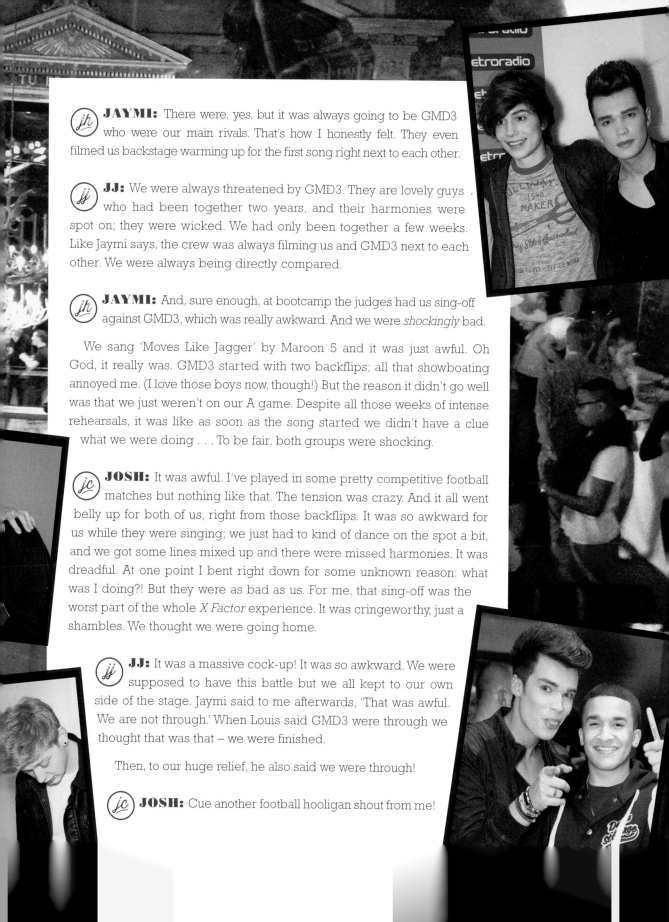

JAYMI: There were, yes, but it was always going to be GMD3 who were our main rivals. That's how I honestly felt. They even filmed us backstage warming up for the first song right next to each other.

JJ: We were always threatened by GMD3. They are lovely guys who had been together two years, and their harmonies were spot on; they were wicked. We had only been together a few weeks. Like Jaymi says, the crew was always filming us and GMD3 next to each other. We were always being directly compared.

JAYMI: And, sure enough, at bootcamp the judges had us sing-off against GMD3, which was really awkward. And we were *shockingly* bad.

We sang 'Moves Like Jagger' by Maroon 5 and it was just awful. Oh God, it really was. GMD3 started with two backflips; all that showboating annoyed me. (I love those boys now, though!) But the reason it didn't go well was that we just weren't on our A game. Despite all those weeks of intense rehearsals, it was like as soon as the song started we didn't have a clue what we were doing . . . To be fair, both groups were shocking.

JOSH: It was awful. I've played in some pretty competitive football matches but nothing like that. The tension was crazy. And it all went belly up for both of us, right from those backflips. It was so awkward for us while they were singing; we just had to kind of dance on the spot a bit, and we got some lines mixed up and there were missed harmonies. It was dreadful. At one point I bent right down for some unknown reason: what was I doing?! But they were as bad as us. For me, that sing-off was the worst part of the whole *X Factor* experience. It was cringeworthy, just a shambles. We thought we were going home.

JJ: It was a massive cock-up! It was so awkward. We were supposed to have this battle but we all kept to our own side of the stage. Jaymi said to me afterwards, 'That was awful. We are not through.' When Louis said GMD3 were through we thought that was that – we were finished.

Then, to our huge relief, he also said we were through!

JOSH: Cue another football hooligan shout from me!

JAYMI: I remember thinking, *How the hell can we get through bootcamp with that shoddy performance?* But somehow they still saw something in us and thankfully we got another chance. What a relief. I almost started to think, *Maybe this is the year after all . . .*

JOSH: There are various websites that publish 'insider gossip' and one of these sites said there was a three-piece boy band called Triple J that had really impressed the judges. I read that and thought, *Oh my God, how cool is this? I am on a website!* Then I logged on a few days later and underneath our feature was an article about GMD3. I feared them. They were a threat, and they had quality vocal harmonies because they had been together for so long.

JAYMI: Like I said, though, I was really buoyed by being sent to the next stage of bootcamp because we weren't very good, so how did we get through? And with all this filming of us and GMD3, it felt different to all the previous times I had been on the show. We were a main feature; they were focusing on us and it felt like they were interested. Whereas before when I'd been at *X Factor* there had been hardly any filming and I'd just faded into insignificance. You can probably tell I analyse everything and strategise. It's how I deal with the situation, I guess, how I prepare.

JJ: So it was back to the hotel to rehearse, rehearse, rehearse. Constantly. Next up was a performance in front of a massive audience, as well as the judges, and we chose to do Guns N' Roses' 'Sweet Child O' Mine'.

JAYMI: Some kids went out partying that night but we didn't, we just practised non-stop. Our choice of song was different. It didn't pay off exactly well, but it helped to show off our voices. We just didn't want to go out there and sing the same old wet ballads.

JOSH: We had long lists of songs that we had to choose from before bootcamp. We went with that iconic rock track because it was just different; no one else was doing that sort of material. And our performance went down really well. We were really happy with it. But the worst bit was that although you want the judges to say something, they don't, and then you walk through the crowd to the back of the arena without any feedback at all. That said, we felt we had done all we could, and we were happy with our performance.

JJ: This is where Mr George Shelley comes into the picture a little bit more. After we'd sang 'Sweet Child O' Mine' George came into a room where both us and GMD3 were practising and he just said to us, 'They are trying to put me in a band. I don't know which one yet, though.' We just said, 'Well, can you sing for us?' and he got out his guitar there and then, and sang to both bands, and we all thought he was wicked. We thought he looked cool too and was a really nice guy. But at that point we couldn't ask him to join. That was not a decision in our hands.

JAYMI: We then headed back to the hotel and we thought we were done with singing at bootcamp, so as it was the 'final' night we went out and I don't mind admitting I had a few drinks. The next morning I woke up with a bit of a sore head and we went to find out who was going to Judges' Houses.

JOSH: We were up at seven in the morning, which made it a long old day in the waiting rooms as it took ages for each category to get sorted out. I was thinking they will put three boy bands in this final six. Then they said two acts were very similar and I *knew* they were talking about us and GMD3. They'd been playing it up to the cameras all week. At that point I thought they were going to put us together as a six-piece. I just wanted to get to Judges' Houses so much. That would have been enough for me to look back in ten years' time and be proud. I was desperate to get there.

JJ: They stood us and GMD3 on stage together, then they really shocked us all by saying they couldn't make their minds up and that they wanted another sing-off, right there and then. We had one minute to choose a song and it had to be completely a cappella. We'd heard GMD3 singing a cappella only the day before and it was really good . . .

JAYMI: Plus, none of us expected to have to sing again. It almost made me feel sick when I heard that. You can see I put my hand across my stomach I was so shocked. My head was spinning, thinking, *No! Don't send me home again!* We had a back-up song, 'Yeah 3x' by Chris Brown, which was, in fact, the only song that we had a cappella. We were dying inside. But I was ready to fight for this.

JOSH: After a tiring week, and with our voices worn out and not warmed up, we didn't expect this. This was unheard of in *X Factor*, this sing-off thing. GMD3 were really confident compared to us. We were crapping ourselves, and we were more interested in what they were going to do, too worried about other people, and so we didn't concentrate on ourselves. We were too reactive. I was also thinking, *This is gonna be shown one hundred per cent. It's gonna be a big feature, so let's just not make a mistake so we won't go home embarrassed. Make ourselves proud.* That's how I felt . . . defeated already.

JAYMI: It wasn't a very good performance. It was a bit random. You pull out all your tricks, but it wasn't ideal. I knew it hadn't gone very well and I knew GMD3 had pulled out a great performance. As soon as we'd finished, I knew we were going home.

from the first line of GMD3's song, when they started with three-piece harmonies, that we were finished. We were only doing two-piece harmonies, so we couldn't compete in that way. They had known those harmonies for years; there was no way we could beat them. I was crying almost straight away. The look on our faces . . . We just knew we were going home.

JAYMI: We knew we were going home. One hundred per cent knew we were going home. In fact, one million per cent positive we were going. Here we go again!

JJ: THE JUDGES DELIBERATED FOR WHAT SEEMED LIKE FOREVER AND THEN GARY TOLD US THE DEVASTATING NEWS. HE SAID WE HAD BEEN NECK AND NECK AND APOLOGISED FOR THE SING-OFF, BUT THEN SAID,

'THE ACT TAKING THE LAST PLACE AT JUDGES' HOUSES FOR THE GROUPS IS GMD3.'

THOSE WORDS STUNG MORE THAN YOU WILL EVER BELIEVE. IT'S SO HORRIBLE TO WATCH THAT CLIP BACK. I WAS ABSOLUTELY DEVASTATED, CRYING, INCONSOLABLE. AND SOMEHOW JAYMI – WHO WAS ALSO COMPLETELY, UTTERLY GUTTED – WALKED OFF THE STAGE AND SHOOK DERMOT'S HAND AND SAID, 'THEY SMASHED IT.' WHAT A GENTLEMAN.

JAYMI: I wasn't jealous of the other band at all. I am not bitter, but I was totally gutted. They deserve to follow their dream and they don't want to see people being bitter and hurtful when they've just had such good news. GMD3/District3 are great lads and we have since become fantastic friends. I was just telling it as I saw it. It was awful for us, though. Josh took it really hard. We all did.

JJ: It was horrible. Waiting for that decision was literally about three minutes, but it felt like an hour. We knew they'd smashed it and we hadn't. We had got friendly with them as well, so it was a horrible situation to be in. I remember the feeling when Gary sent us home. It was horrid, absolutely gutted.

JOSH: The worst thing was they came off and they were really gracious, bless 'em. They were already filming us and we were shattered, crying and all that, but then obviously GMD3 were delighted, so when they filmed them they did this big 'Woo-hoo!' – which they were perfectly entitled to and well deserved . . . but you can just see us in the background, crumpled and absolutely gutted.

GEORGE: I wasn't aware of any of this at the time. I'd bumped into the boys a couple of times, as JJ has explained, but initially I was concentrating on getting through myself. At first I was paired up for bootcamp with a Justin Bieber lookalike with a great voice and this young black guy called Leon, who was amazing as well. They were both really good vocally. I just thought I stood no chance. You have to then select a song you all agree on and I was really naive because I chose a song that I liked rather than the one that suited my voice the most. I should have gone with Kings of Leon, but I went for Kelly Clarkson's 'Stronger' just because I loved it! We all had individual lines to sing and we spent the whole night working together; they were nice lads and we worked well as a team, unlike a few of the groups that you saw arguing at bootcamp!

I opened the performance up and we sang it an octave below because it's a high girl's song but Gary wasn't impressed. He said, 'Why did you pick that song? It's not suited for any of your voices, it's an octave below and it's very boring. Sorry, guys, you are going home.' And that was that. Booted out. Day one. Gone.

Or so I thought.

I walked off stage but before I really had a chance to think about it, one of the researchers pulled me aside and said, 'Come with me, George, an exec wants to speak to you.' I went to see a producer, who told me they wanted to put me in a group. I was up for that because the alternative was going home and being left with nothing. I was like, *Yes! A lifeline!* I went crazy!

I spent all that night waiting to be put into a group. Eventually they sent me into a room alone and then one by one a girl came in, then a boy, then a girl, then a boy, and it became obvious that we were being put into a mixed group. I was really excited, I don't mind admitting. Absolutely chuffed.

The next day we did some filming, then afterwards Tulisa came up to me out of the blue and she kinda cornered me on my own and said, 'There's two boy bands out there for you. I suggest you go and have a look at them and see what you think. Speak with them. I think you'd do really well in a boy band.' I was really confused by now, but I did as she suggested and went to find out these two bands she'd spoken about, GMD3 and Triple J.

This was what JJ was talking about earlier, when I ended up playing my guitar and singing in front of both bands in that room. As he has already said, GMD3 and Triple J were in this room together and they were both eyeing each other up, having a chat. They looked at me and said, 'All right, mate, what's your story?' I explained to them and said about the two boy bands, and they said, 'Come on then, let's hear you.' So I had to get my guitar out in front of both bands and basically audition! They all said I looked cool and had a good voice.

I went home and explained to my family that I could be put into a mixed group or I could join one of these two boy bands. The next day I was left to my own devices in the arena until about one o'clock. I was waiting around and I didn't see either Triple J or GMD3. Then they told me the six-piece mixed group was going to try out as two three-piece mixed groups, so I was sent off with these guys called AJ and Charley, who were very cool.

All of that day we were practising in vocal workshops and then late in the afternoon they added another member to try out, an amazing girl called Megan. (Bootcamp is like this, there's a lot of experimenting and trying out various people you enjoy singing with.) By now we only had two hours to get our song down, which was 'Earthquake' by Labrinth. You don't find out their decision until the next day but I thought we had done quite well.

The next day my four-piece was up on stage with the other contestants waiting to find out who was going to Judges' Houses. You are standing on stage and it's just the worst feeling in the world, so nerve-wracking. You are looking at the judges, trying to read their minds. Nicole looked at me and then looked away at the floor and I thought, *She knows I am going home*, then Gary did the same. My legs turned to jelly, everything was in slow motion, they started calling out names who were through and with every act that got called, my heart was sinking. Then it was down to the last place at Judges' Houses and they called out Rough Copy.

Gary said, 'Sorry, guys, for the rest of you the journey ends here.'

Those are the worst words I think I have ever heard in my life!

I WAS OUT OF X FACTOR.

I headed backstage, totally dejected, and that's when I saw Triple J again. I went up this escalator and bumped into them at the top and they looked completely gutted too. They told me that they hadn't made it to Judges' Houses either.

JJ gave me a couple of their phone numbers and said, 'Best of luck, George . . . Let's stay in touch.'

'GEORGE: THE NEXT DAY WE DID SOME FILMING, THEN AFTERWARDS TULISA CAME UP TO ME OUT OF THE BLUE AND SHE KINDA CORNERED ME ON MY OWN AND SAID, "THERE'S TWO BOY BANDS OUT THERE FOR YOU. I SUGGEST YOU GO AND HAVE A LOOK AT THEM AND SEE WHAT YOU THINK. SPEAK WITH THEM. I THINK YOU'D DO REALLY WELL IN A BOY BAND." I WAS REALLY CONFUSED BY NOW, BUT I DID AS SHE SUGGESTED AND WENT TO FIND OUT THESE TWO BANDS SHE'D SPOKEN ABOUT, GMD3 AND TRIPLE J.'

LIFE IS A
ROLLERCOASTER

JAYMI: AFTER WE HAD LOST THE SING-OFF AND THEY SENT GMD3 TO JUDGES' HOUSES, I JUST WANTED TO GET HOME AS FAST AS I COULD. I'D HAD ENOUGH. I WANTED TO GET HOME TO MY FAMILY. I WAS LIKE,

I AM DONE!

THIS IS IT, LITERALLY. NO MORE. NEVER EVER AGAIN WILL I TRY TO DO THIS SHOW, OR TRY TO MAKE IT. I AM GOING HOME.

Then I lost my bag on the train on my way home, which had my laptop in it, as well as my phone, my passport, my wallet and all my jewellery. I lost everything. I remember that feeling like it was the worst day of my life.

I got back to Luton and I really had had enough then. I had no job, no career, no laptop, no phone, nothing. I'd even lost my house because I couldn't afford to keep it, so I just said, *Enough is enough, I am going to be a teacher. That is the end of it.* I was done and I was happy to say that.

I don't mind admitting I went home and picked up the nearest bottle of alcohol but really quickly a feeling of calm came over me because I just thought, *Okay, I have given up now. This is it. I am done.*

It was weird, I genuinely didn't wanna do music and singing any more, so I wasn't as devo'd as the year before. I said to myself, *I have a fantastic boyfriend, an amazing relationship, an amazing family. I am not hard up. There are always people worse off out there. I am not dying!* So I was gutted, yes, but I also thought, *Get up and get on with it. You just need to move on.*

JOSH: IT WAS SUCH A BLOODY LONG WAY BACK ON THE TRAIN FROM LIVERPOOL. WHEN I GOT BACK TO ASCOT, I JUST WENT BACK TO MUM'S. I COULDN'T BEAR TO BE ON MY OWN. I THINK I CRIED THE WHOLE AFTERNOON. I WAS ABSOLUTELY GUTTED. I WAS DONE WITH MUSIC AND THIS WAS THE END OF MY SINGING. I KNOW THAT SOUNDS EXTREME BUT AFTER FIVE YEARS OF TRYING TO BE IN A BOY BAND, DOING LOADS OF DIFFERENT PROJECTS THAT HAD ALL FAILED, I JUST COULDN'T BRING MYSELF TO TRY AGAIN.

Going back to work was really hard. That first day sat back at my desk was tough, I just sat there staring at the ceiling, thinking, *I can't do this*. It was frustrating for me because I suddenly looked at my job differently and realised it was not what I wanted to do any more. This *X Factor* experience had changed my perspective on my job, which was quite bad really. (To try to relax I would spend a lot of time at my friend's horse yard, which I loved and still do.) I absolutely know my situation back then was not rock bottom compared to what a lot of people go through, of course not, but in terms of my ambitions and my hopes for a singing career, this was my dream being shattered.

This next part is quite embarrassing, but I am going to be completely honest with you here. I couldn't tell people at work that I hadn't got through. I said we were still waiting to find out. I couldn't bring myself to actually say the words. As soon as I said that I thought, *You have just lied, why did you do that?* But do you know what? I couldn't bring myself to tell them for another week. I was devastated. Part of me wanted to paint this picture in my head that somehow there was still a glimmer of hope, that something might still happen. But it couldn't . . . could it?

JJ: I went back to my job working with horses and I felt horrible. People were asking me how I had got on and it was just gutting having to keep saying we never made it. People had been taking the mick out of me being in a boy band so when we'd got through to bootcamp it had felt great, but then we got kicked out anyway. I had so wanted to prove a point, to show that if you want to do something in life you can do it – just work hard and try. The first week back I was sick. I couldn't sleep properly. Josh and Jaymi were the same.

JAYMI: Absolutely, all three of us were under the weather. And yet something in the back of my head was telling me that this wasn't it for us and *X Factor*. At first when I got that feeling I assumed it was just wishful thinking so I pushed it aside. But that feeling kept coming back . . . maybe it is not over yet? I don't know why I thought that, but I did.

JJ: That's weird because I thought exactly the same. I had a gut feeling this was not the end. No reason, no justification, just a weird feeling. It can't be the end, can it? And even more weirdly, my dad kept saying to me, 'You are going back, there's a twist, you watch.' Surely not?

JOSH: While I was trying to pick myself up after bootcamp, I'd sent a few emails to some researchers on *X Factor* that we'd got to know, just to say thank you for the opportunity and wishing them all the best. They emailed back to wish us well too but then about two weeks later this one particular researcher I knew quite well actually rang me. I was at work, and I was still really down, not myself at all. Anyway, this researcher said that ITV2 wanted to come and do some filming, to see what we had been up to since bootcamp; I thought that was a bit odd, and I also thought, *There isn't much to film!* Because although we'd said we would carry on and put a few clips up on YouTube and all that, we hadn't actually made any progress as a band yet, we were still licking our wounds.

Then he called again and said, 'Are you and the boys available today?' I explained that we were all at work and that we lived in three distant locations so that wasn't possible, but then he mentioned three or four days coming up and said, 'Can you keep these dates free at the end of August, please?'

So now I was intrigued. On the one hand, I thought it was more exposure so it couldn't do us any harm, but on the other I had a funny feeling, just a gut feeling that something was going on. A seed had been planted. Maybe . . . ?

SO I RANG THE BOYS . . .

JAYMI: So I get this phone call saying *X Factor* want us back for some more filming. They've said Olly Murs is going to come and film at Josh's house. I was like, *No, that can't be. They are messing with us. It's just for telly*. I will be honest here and say at that stage I really couldn't have cared less, I was so angry. Angry at what had happened and just angry at life in general, knowing I'd wanted it for so long but I wasn't going to get a break. I had had enough. So I didn't want to even go that day. I'd lost *all* interest. I hadn't sung once since bootcamp, not even at home. I can't believe I am saying this, but at that precise moment there was not a part of me that loved music and singing any more.

JJ: While I was at work in the yard I got the call from Josh about the filming and Olly going round his house. I checked the Internet and saw that Olly was just back off tour in America (he hadn't been at bootcamp), so that checked out, but I wasn't convinced. Something was up. I said that to Dad and he was like, 'That's not normal, why would they do that?'

JAYMI: So I dragged myself to go to this stupid filming, down to Josh's house, and as I drove over there, a little part of me thought, *Maybe they are going to call us back?* So I looked on Twitter for Olly Murs and he was indeed going to rejected contestants' homes to see how they had got on in recent weeks. *Okay, so maybe that's all it is, after all.*

JOSH: My whole mental attitude had changed. I'd had a glimmer of hope, even though there wasn't any hope to have really: it was just ITV2 filming. On the day of filming the boys came round here, then the camera crew arrived and set up, and we were all waiting for Olly. I was looking at this crew and then I said, 'Hang on, you guys don't work for ITV2, do you?' and they said, 'Yeah, we do sometimes, er, yeah,' but I didn't recognise them from previous filming, I thought they worked for ITV1, which would have meant something was going on with the main show. Meanwhile, my mum and sister were sat in the car outside my house, waiting to get Olly Murs's autograph!

> **'JAYMI:** SO I DRAGGED MYSELF TO GO TO THIS STUPID FILMING, DOWN TO JOSH'S HOUSE, AND AS I DROVE OVER THERE, A LITTLE PART OF ME THOUGHT, **MAYBE THEY ARE GOING TO CALL US BACK?'**

JJ: Then the film crew said, 'Right, Olly is two minutes away. Let's get the cameras ready,' and they sat us down and put mikes on us. Josh was actually messing about, taking the mick, saying, 'Hey, boys, what if Louis Walsh comes in here and says they've made a massive mistake and they want us after all!' We all just laughed and told him to stop being silly.

JAYMI: Yeah, we did, but I was starting to think he might be right. There was just a feeling . . .

JOSH: THEN THERE WAS A KNOCK AT THE DOOR. I WALKED UP TO LET OLLY IN, BUT WHEN I OPENED IT LOUIS WALSH WAS STANDING THERE! I WAS SO SHOCKED, I HELD OUT MY HAND REALLY FORMALLY AND SAID, 'HI, LOUIS. I AM JOSH. NICE TO MEET YOU.' IT WAS REALLY COMICAL, BUT AS I SHOOK HIS HAND, I KNEW . . .

JAYMI: It was the best feeling when Louis turned up because we all knew what that meant. In that instant, everything came flooding back, *everything.* I was like, *OMG!* All those good feelings about singing and music came rushing back. He didn't say anything at this point, we still had to do the filming, so we all sat down on the sofa and Louis started telling us all about what had happened. A band had been kicked out and there was now a free slot. He was really building up to this big reveal . . . but I knew, and I was just thinking, *Come on, Louis, just tell us! We are going to Judges' Houses! Just say it!*

JOSH: We were sitting there like little nervous children, and then he said it, 'Boys, you are going to Judges' Houses' . . . and we just went crazy. I started crying – surprise, surprise! – but the relief. I couldn't believe it. Amazing feeling!

JAYMI: As much as I knew he was going to say that, when he actually did I didn't believe him! I was like, *What?!*

JJ: We screamed so loudly, I'm surprised Josh's house was still standing! It was amazing, and one of the best highlights of my life to hear those words, knowing we'd got another chance. Afterwards, I rang my mum and dad. 'Dad, you were right . . .'

JOSH: Louis left after being at my place for only about twenty minutes, and we were all sat there again, just the three of us, shell-shocked. Then my phone beeped and it was a text from Mum that for some reason, network problems or whatever, had been delayed. She was trying to tip me off because it said, 'Josh, Louis Walsh is outside the house at the door!'

JAYMI: I had just resigned myself to not doing this any more, then this curveball gets thrown in. We were absolutely ecstatic. I knew GMD3 were still going and I knew they had beaten us once already, so part of me still thought, *How the hell are we going to beat them again?* Maybe we were there just to fill out the numbers? We had less than two weeks to prepare for Judges' Houses.

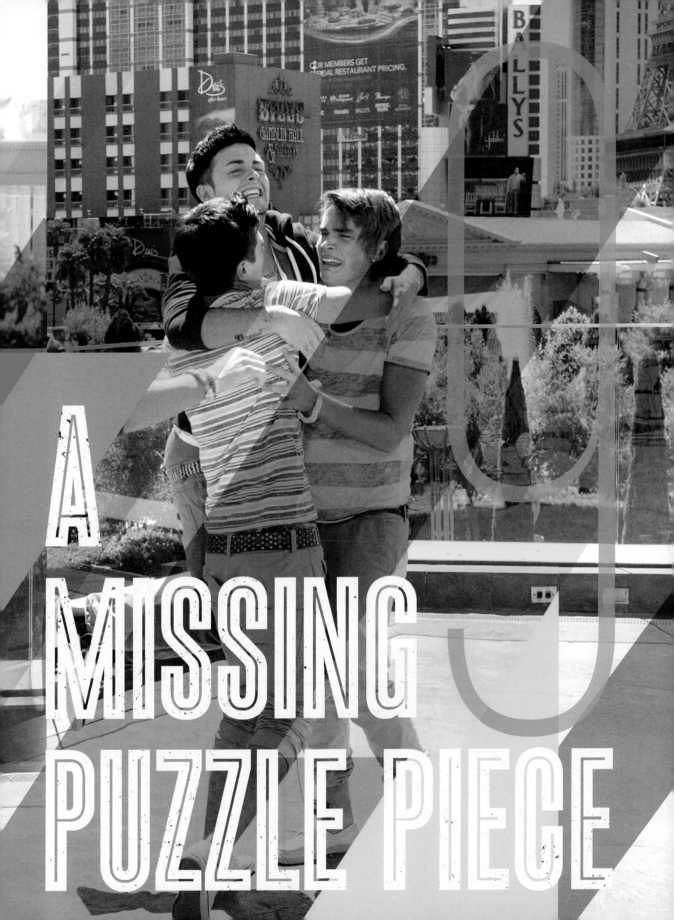

GEORGE: My life after bootcamp was a crazy whirlwind, so much happened in so little time. I'd had that rejection and gone home gutted, but the band I was in were resolved to continue and we had various meetings with management companies and researched prospective labels and all that. There were a couple of line-up changes and it was all a bit up in the air, but I was determined to make something work (one particular girl who was involved, called Parisa, has since become one of my closest friends). I had even arranged to book some studio time and record some demos. I was really focused, full-on fighting for this. I didn't want this to be the end.

During the very first day that I'd had on my own after bootcamp, I was just spending time at home with my family and Emily, chilling back in Clevedon. I was actually making my bed when my phone went off but I didn't get to it in time; it was from a blocked number. I remember thinking, *That's odd*, because it was only ever *X Factor* who called me on a blocked number. Why would *X Factor* be calling me? Perhaps there's some forms I forgot to fill in?

This blocked number rang again straight away so I answered it this time and it was a really nice researcher that I knew from the show. She asked after me and I told her I'd been trying a few band ideas and all that and then she said, 'I bet you were gutted when you didn't get through bootcamp?'

'Er, yes! You could say that, I was completely gutted.'

'RIGHT . . . WELL, GEORGE, HOW WOULD YOU LIKE TO GO TO JUDGES' HOUSES?'

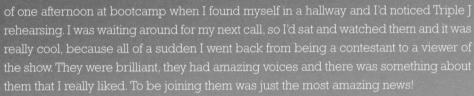

I was in shock. I literally ran out of the front door, straight across the road and came to a stop on the pavement opposite my house, just picking leaves off this random bush! She explained that they wanted to recall me and put me in a group and that I had to leave in a few days for the Judges' Houses.

When I heard it was Triple J that they were putting me with, *I was so excited!* At that exact moment I had a flashback of one afternoon at bootcamp when I found myself in a hallway and I'd noticed Triple J rehearsing. I was waiting around for my next call, so I'd sat and watched them and it was really cool, because all of a sudden I went back from being a contestant to a viewer of the show. They were brilliant, they had amazing voices and there was something about them that I really liked. To be joining them was just the most amazing news!

It was hard to leave behind the mixed group I had been working with because I had become really close friends with them, but I knew this was an opportunity that was too good to miss.

JJ: So shortly after Louis had told us the news that we were going to Judges' Houses, I got a text from George, completely out of the blue and it just said, 'Crap!' That was weird. Why would you send a text just saying, 'Crap!'? Then Josh phoned me and said, 'JJ, I've just had a text from George and all it says is, "Crap!"' So we phoned him up.

JOSH: We got hold of George and he said *X Factor* wanted him to be in our band. Now, remember at Bootcamp when he had sung in front of us and GMD3? Well, we said there and then that he was wicked and would really suit a boy band, so we were like, 'Cool! Sounds like a brilliant idea!' Funnily enough, after we had lost to GMD3, we had even spoken briefly about how it felt like something was missing. The reason we never got through was because we weren't good enough as a three-piece. So maybe George was the answer?

JAYMI: George came to Josh's and we were all there waiting for him to walk in, which was a strange moment, but we got on brilliantly straight away. When we'd met George at bootcamp we loved him already. *X Factor* got it bang on. George never felt like an outsider to us; it just wasn't like that. He was instantly a part of the band. I remember looking at us as a band on that day when we first all got together and thinking, *This is right. We are ready!* Straight away there was an instant click with George. It was destined from day one. I was ecstatic.

'**JJ:** I GOT A TEXT FROM GEORGE, COMPLETELY OUT OF THE BLUE AND IT JUST SAID, "**CRAP!**" THAT WAS WEIRD.'

JJ: Being completely honest, initially there was a concern: *Does he look too young?* But as soon as we got to know him that was irrelevant. He just slotted in perfectly, and we loved him.

GEORGE: They were really nice to me. That first meeting was a big deal for me. I was still paranoid about how young I looked and I didn't have many mates who were older lads. Most of my friends were girls, so all of a sudden I was chatting with these twenty-something lads and it was quite daunting. But they quickly put me at ease and we hit it off really quickly.

JOSH: That five days before Judges' Houses was a massive bonding process. George stayed at mine, we also stayed in London, we rehearsed, we hung out together. Everyone else in the show was preparing to go to Judges' Houses but we were trying to bond as well, because we didn't really know each other. George really did fit in straight away. It must have been hard for him to come in with these three quite big personalities, but we just clicked. If you step back from the George situation, I was new to the other boys as well. We didn't really know each other that well yet; the whole band had only been going a few months.

JJ: We rehearsed like mad, hours and hours every day. There was just no way that we could turn up there unprepared so we really put the hours in.

JAYMI: I was ecstatic. There weren't any other made-up groups this year and from knowing the show and watching it for so many years and studying how they worked, I knew they had seen something in us, something different. They were now investing time and energy in us. I remember thinking, *This is good. This is my break. This is lucky for us!*

GEORGE: I didn't even have a suitcase! I brought all my clothes up in a holdall. I wasn't prepared for Judges' Houses one bit. My mum and Nan were like, 'What?! You are going to Judges' Houses?!' While we were waiting to fly out, I researched GMD3 because they were my competition now and I could see they were amazing. We were definitely the underdogs.

JJ: We arrived at the airport and there were seven groups so it was fierce competition. Then we opened our tickets and it said we were flying to Vegas! Wow! Everyone wants to go to Vegas!

JAYMI: I was a bit groggy while we were waiting for Judges' Houses. I wasn't well, so I was on antibiotics and painkillers but they weren't working and they were making my throat dry and my mouth blistered. My sleep wasn't right and I wasn't eating properly, and yet I was supposed to be going to America to sing in front of the judges. I just remember being a bit of a disaster, not feeling a hundred per cent.

But at the same time I was ecstatic about getting through. We had been through enough pain, we had struggled for this, this was our reward. I felt that if you make Judges' Houses, then when you come home you can gig, you can get work. I just wanted to start making a living. There's a chance you could get signed and that was as far as I needed to go in my head. I really felt like we could be the next big boy band.

JOSH: The day before we were flying out to Vegas we still didn't have a name confirmed for the band. We thought of The Lost Boys, someone else mentioned Boyfriend, and Brick Lane and Ace were also put forward. Then we got talking about being proud of being British, someone said United Jacks and I think it was George who suggested Union Jacks. Then Jaymi came out with Union J!

'**JJ :** THE DAY BEFORE WE WERE FLYING OUT TO VEGAS WE STILL DIDN'T HAVE A NAME CONFIRMED FOR THE BAND. WE THOUGHT OF THE LOST BOYS, SOMEONE ELSE MENTIONED BOYFRIEND, AND BRICK LANE AND ACE WERE ALSO PUT FORWARD. THEN WE GOT TALKING ABOUT BEING PROUD OF BEING BRITISH, SOMEONE SAID UNITED JACKS AND I THINK IT WAS GEORGE WHO SUGGESTED UNION JACKS. THEN JAYMI CAME OUT WITH

UNION J!'

GEORGE: Arriving in Vegas was like walking into a massive hairdryer – this constant dry heat. Then it dawns on you what you are doing. We didn't know who our judge was at this point, so we went to this luxurious five-star hotel to wait. It was so surreal. Five days before I'd been on my own in Clevedon and now I was sharing a room with Josh in this exclusive hotel in Las Vegas, about to sing to the judges. How could *X Factor* mess with my mind any more?!

We all went out on a limo ride round Vegas, which was filmed and a lot of fun, then we went to meet our judge. By now it was dark but still boiling hot, and we were standing there waiting when all of a sudden this limo pulled up and we were all really tense waiting to see which judge it was . . . and out popped an Elvis impersonator! We were all laughing, then Elvis opened the other door and Louis Walsh jumped out! And then Sharon Osbourne!

JAYMI: I was really homesick because I'd never been away from my boyfriend like that before and obviously there was a lot of pressure on us because, as Josh says, this was going to be our first ever performance as a four-piece! But at the same time I knew *X Factor* wanted us to do well. They had decided that we were special and that was enough for me. Everyone else in the category was so good, I was thinking, *Why can't you be rubbish?! Give us a chance!* It was all a bit of a blur, such a lot to take in, but I remember loving it and loving my life at that moment.

JJ: We arrived on the Thursday and we were singing on the Saturday evening, performing Carly Rae Jepsen's 'Call Me Maybe'. At first we were thinking a cappella, and there was a piano available, but in the end we got George to play the guitar so it was different. We were happy with this song but when we listened to the previous performances, the other acts were smashing it.

JOSH: REMEMBER, THIS WAS OUR VERY FIRST TIME SINGING TO SOMEONE AS A FOUR-PIECE AND HERE WE WERE, ON A HOTEL ROOFTOP IN LAS VEGAS, IN BURNING HEAT, STANDING TEN FEET FROM LOUIS WALSH AND SHARON OSBOURNE! THAT'S NOT WEIRD AT ALL, IS IT?!

JJ: Not weird at all! You're right, though. I remember coming down the stairs to see Louis and Sharon on that hotel rooftop, and despite my nerves I was thinking, *Not many people in the world get to stand on a rooftop in Vegas and sing to those two!* What an experience!

JOSH: THE AIR WAS SO DRY, THOUGH, WASN'T IT, JJ?! MY THROAT WAS BONE DRY. I DO REMEMBER VIVIDLY THAT JUST BEFORE WE WALKED OUT SUDDENLY SOMETHING CLICKED, SOMETHING CAME TOGETHER. FOR THE FIRST TIME EVER I WAS IN A GROUP THAT FELT COMPLETELY NATURAL. I HAD A FEELING THIS COULD REALLY WORK AND I THOUGHT, **THIS IS OUR CHANCE! LET'S DO THIS!**

GEORGE: As we performed the song we watched everything the judges did: all their facial expressions, every time they looked this way or that you tried to read everything.

JJ: We were happy and kind of had fun with it. George had a key role in it, which was wicked and quite deliberate on our part; it was us announcing that he was very much a member of our band. The two judges were smiling and Sharon was nodding her head to the beat, so it seemed to go quite well. They don't give you any feedback at all, though.

JAYMI: We'd also had to perform another song for ITV2, which was 'Forever Young'. I was happy with how 'Call Me Maybe' came across, but 'Forever Young' was just okay. However, I think given the circumstances we did pretty well. We went upstairs after 'Call Me Maybe' and went absolutely bonkers. We were so happy, I don't think we were cocky, but, you know, we smashed that. I had the realisation that if we are that *ready* after three days, imagine what we would be like in a year! That was so exciting.

GEORGE: As Sharon walked away she said, 'They are cute, aren't they?' That was the only snippet of feedback that we heard. You then go back to the hotel and have the *longest* night of your life waiting to find out! *Have we done it?* We went to bed quite hopeful.

JAYMI: Then literally in the space of half an hour everything switched to reverse. You worry, you panic, you overthink. All those good feelings from the performance disappeared and it was just anxiety for twenty-four hours.

JJ: On the morning of the results I rang up Mum. I was that nervous. I slept fine but if I talked about the results I would start to cry. I just didn't wanna get this close and be rejected, like so many rejections before. We all knew that feeling. Mum said to stay positive . . . but I wasn't convinced we were gonna make it.

JOSH: That day was horrible, I remember having to do some interviews about an hour before we were told, before our fate was set. Every time I spoke I was holding back the tears. I get my emotional side from my mum, but I don't really care what people think. And my God, it was so emotional.

GEORGE: We were just sitting in this room for what seemed like hours. We sat in silence much of the time, or chatting about our chances nervously. Jaymi said he thought we were through, and I was like, 'Don't jinx it!' But he was like, 'No, we are through . . . I feel really positive this time.'

JAYMI: Waiting around to find out the result was painful! I remember how much *more* it meant to me then than it had ever done before. I'd gone from being switched off to singing altogether a few days earlier to never wanting anything so much in my entire life. The waiting made me sick to my stomach. There were three boy bands who were clearly the main contenders: us, GMD3 and an older group called Times Red, who were really nice guys too.

They started calling bands up to find out their fate and when we didn't go first I started worrying and trying to work out the order of events. *So, they will go through, then the next lot will be out, so if they are called next we could be fourth . . . but then that means we'd probably be sent home . . .* It was madness! You don't know what decision was made for other bands because they are taken out a different way, so you don't see them again. You really are left in the dark, second-guessing like crazy. Then they called GMD3 out to get their results. For me, to see them go first meant we were going home.

GEORGE:

WHEN GMD3 WENT THROUGH, I THOUGHT TO MYSELF

WHOEVER THEY CALL NEX IS GOING HOME . . .

THEN THE RESEARCHER SHOUTED,

'UNION J, YOU'RE UP NEX

JJ: As soon as they said we were next, I literally broke down. George was holding me up, I was shaking, absolutely shaking. It was horrible. The worst emotional experience I've ever gone through in my career. We walked out to see Louis sitting there, ready to tell us his decision. It was baking hot. The heat was so intense.

JOSH: We were all drinking water to keep calm, trying to find ways to cope with the nerves. We got to the rooftop and waited for Louis to be ready to film, then finally stood in front of him in that searing heat to learn our fate. I was breathing frantically as he began to speak and he started by saying how well George had fitted into the picture, but then he also said there were other groups in the competition who 'had the edge'. But then a helicopter flew over and they had to stop filming and start all over again. He started saying the same things and then as we got ready for the decision a police siren blared out in the background, so we had to start all over again. It was just *unbearable*.

GEORGE: Eight times we had to re-start. It was horrendous! And Louis had his sunglasses on, so even between takes we couldn't read his thoughts. I was finding it really hard to breathe, sandwiched in between Josh and JJ, hugging them round their waists. After a couple of re-starts, JJ started crying and shaking, and was literally having to hold him up.

JAYMI: Josh was the same! He was sagging under the heat and the nervous exhaustion of all these re-starts. Then finally Louis was able to tell us his decision

'Guys, we loved your first audition. We saw great potential and in the sing-off that's when you showed a little bit of spark, a little bit of potential.'

WE ARE THROUGH!

'George, putting you in was a bit of a gamble . . .'

WE ARE GOING HOME!

'I think you've fitted in very, very well in the band . . .'

NO, HANG ON, WE ARE THROUGH!

'But there's an awful lot of work to be done and we haven't got months, guys. We have only got weeks . . .'

NOPE, WE ARE GOING HOME.

'The problem is, boys, there are other boy bands in the competition and they have the edge on this group, because they have been together longer.'

OKAY, SO WE ARE DEFINITELY GOING HOME NOW . . .

'I have thought long and hard about this, guys . . . Guys, we are in Vegas . . . but I am not a gambling man . . .'

AH, NO, THAT'S IT, WE ARE FINISHED . . .

'Until today!'

WHAT DID HE JUST SAY?

'You are through!'

JOSH: THERE WAS A PAUSE OF FOUR SECONDS WHILE
LOUIS'S WORDS SUNK IN, WHICH IS WHY HE ALMOST
HAD TO REPEAT HIMSELF AND SHOUT,

'YOU ARE THROUGH!'

WE JUST EXPLODED! WHOA! I COULDN'T EVEN RUN TO LOUIS.
I FELL TO MY KNEES WITH MY HEAD IN MY HANDS WHILE
THE OTHER THREE LADS JUST DIVE-BOMBED LOUIS!

GEORGE: We jumped on Louis and pummelled him. Completely flattened him!

JOSH: To think you are going to be performing on live TV in front of ten million people every week. By achieving that I had done everything I wanted to. Out of the whole *X Factor* experience, there was no experience like that moment. It's probably also the best feeling of my life ever!

JAYMI: I'd probably agree with you, Josh. Getting through Judges' Houses was the best thing. My favourite feeling of the whole experience, I think. When I watch the clip back now, it is still so exciting. We cry so much but it's such an emotional experience! I've never been so nervous in my entire life ever, ever, ever! Wow, what a feeling! I will never forget that moment. If I am ever down or feeling fed up, I should watch that clip back. The best day of my life, career-wise. A pivotal moment.

JJ: Mental. Best feeling of my life. Full stop. We absolutely floored Louis! For me that point was like, I had done something in my life that I could look back on in years to come and be proud of.

GEORGE: I'd promised myself I wouldn't cry and during the filming of the decision itself I didn't, but as we walked down the stairway after Louis had told us the amazing news I burst out crying. I was in floods of tears; I've never cried that much, I couldn't breathe. By then the other boys had got the tears out of their system, they'd cried as much as they could, but it suddenly hit me! I felt like I was having a panic attack, and the boys calmed me down, then wave after wave of excitement and happiness just swept over us. We had done it! I couldn't believe it!

JOSH: When Louis said, 'You are through!' we became four. We were a unit from that moment. For me, anyway, that was when Union J arrived. We had been through such an emotional experience together as a four-piece, and that bonds you and brings you closer together.

JAYMI: It was just the best feeling ever; I was *so* ready for what was coming next. In my mind I had Louis Walsh's last words to us on that hotel rooftop ringing in my head: 'Right, the work starts now. You have got a lot of competition, and you are never gonna get this chance again . . . and, by the way, don't let me down!'

UNION J WERE GOING TO THE LIVE FINALS!

THE
LIVE FINALS

AYMI: About three hours after we found out the Judges' Houses results we were sitting on a flight back to England. I remember being so happy because I didn't have to do a ten-hour flight with a no from Louis. I was ill. My mouth was really swollen, I was run–down and physically I was spent. They'd messed the tickets up and I ended up in the back seat of the plane but I was as happy as Larry. I didn't care, we were going to the finals! I have to admit, I did have the odd drink or two to celebrate!

JJ: We were so tired on that flight back, but the adrenalin pulls you through it all. We weren't allowed to phone our family from Vegas with the good news. In fact, I think they took our phones off us to make sure! What an amazing feeling it was flying home ready to tell your parents that news! Our parents were all called ahead of our landing and told to meet us at the airport, where we were filmed running out for the big 'reveal'. And everybody went crazy! I remember in among all the cheering and crying and sheer happiness, I thought about my grandad and I wished he could have been there to see what I had done. I know he would have been very proud of me.

Anyway, the day after we landed it was back to work at the stables again while we prepared for the finals. I still had to earn some money!

JAYMI: When we got back, it coincided with our original auditions being broadcast and there were a few people at home who made snide comments, but I knew it was just jealousy. I didn't need to bite back. I just thought, *You were an idiot your whole life about me and my singing, and now I have this there's no need to answer you, I will just smile.* I didn't need to lower myself.

While we were preparing for the live finals it started to dawn on me that we'd be fighting it out every week, singing in front of millions of people. The enormity of what we had achieved and also what we were facing started to sink in. But we were so ready for it – this was what I'd been waiting for all my life and we rehearsed day and night, literally.

'**JAYMI:** WHILE WE WERE PREPARING FOR THE LIVE FINALS IT STARTED TO DAWN ON ME THAT WE'D BE FIGHTING IT OUT EVERY WEEK, SINGING IN FRONT OF MILLIONS OF PEOPLE. THE ENORMITY OF WHAT WE HAD ACHIEVED AND ALSO WHAT WE WERE FACING STARTED TO SINK IN. BUT WE WERE SO READY FOR IT – THIS WAS WHAT I'D BEEN WAITING FOR ALL MY LIFE AND WE REHEARSED DAY AND NIGHT, LITERALLY.'

GEORGE: Ahead of the first show in Week 1 we all had meetings with the TV production team and then the contestants moved into the Corinthia hotel, in London. Straight away I bumped into a few faces I recognised, such as Ella, James and Lucy Spraggan, and there was a really nice celebratory atmosphere. I'd never been to many hotels and now I was going to live for weeks (sharing with Josh) in this five-star place, whereas I'm just used to my tiny three-bedroom house in Clevedon.

By then there were only two weeks till the first live show, which were a blur of rehearsals, makeovers, tans, eyebrows being done, haircuts, teeth whitening, facials – they get you TV prepped. Then you do all the glamour shots for the opening credits . . . Oh, and Josh had his quiff done!

JOSH: Thank you, George! Yes, I did have my hair cut, which was quite a big thing for me, from having long hair to being a lot shorter. But that was the least of my worries. Week 1 was Olympic-themed and for us it was a disaster.

GEORGE: We were going to do ABBA's 'The Winner Takes It All' and when we rehearsed it sounded good, but then at the last minute someone decided to change it to Queen's 'Don't Stop Me Now'.

JJ: We were rehearsing and other people sounded so good, but ours sounded rubbish. Before we went on stage I didn't get nervous, I was really excited. It felt so exhilarating to finally go on to the *X Factor* stage, where the biggest artists worldwide have performed, and where we were about to sing in front of ten million people.

'**GEORGE:** WE WERE PERCHED ON THIS BOX AND THE BAND NAME WAS WRITTEN ACROSS THE BOTTOM, BUT TO ME, THAT NIGHT IT WAS JUST NOT RIGHT AT ALL. WE ONLY HAD ONE BIT OF CHOREOGRAPHY, TO MOVE THE MIKE STANDS, BUT EVEN THAT LOOKED RUBBISH. WE FELT AND LOOKED SO RESTRICTED ON THAT BOX. THE WHOLE PERFORMANCE JUST WASN'T WHAT WE IMAGINED OURSELVES TO BE.'

JOSH: We walked out on t[o] that iconic stage and we wer[e] so excited . . . but not for long! The song wasn't right. We'd struggled a[t] the start of the week and they'd eve[n] brought in Brian Friedman to give us [a] lift and help us with the choreograph[y] On the night we were swamped b[y] all the dancers, we were wooden, w[e] sang badly, everything was wrong.

JAYMI: It was horrific. O[h] God! People say I am harsh o[n] myself sometimes, that I have ver[y] high standards, but let me tell yo[u] Week 1 was horrific. It's iconic playing there, of course. It's an amazing venu[e] but we seriously messed up. I ha[d] laryngitis so I had not sung properl[y] for the whole week, but that wasn't the problem. We sang badly, we looke[d] wrong, there was too much productio[n] and no one was feeling it.

GEORGE: We were perche[d] on this box and the band nam[e] was written across the bottom, but t[o] me, as a graphic-design student, i[t] looked terrible. The production staf[f] work so incredibly hard on that sho[w] you wouldn't believe how hard, bu[t] that night it was just not right at all. We only had one bit of choreography, t[o] move the mike stands, but even tha[t] looked rubbish. We felt and looke[d] so restricted on that box. The whol[e] performance just wasn't what we imagined ourselves to be.

JOSH: We got quite negative comments from the judges, although mainly about the song choice and Tulisa especially blamed Louis for that. However, this didn't distract from the fact we were so bad. George came up to me immediately afterwards and said, 'We are so going home.' I couldn't disagree. We were the worst out of everyone. You can see that on our faces when we have finished.

JJ: The comments after were absolutely terrible. It was out of tune. I don't even wanna put it on YouTube and watch it! Tulisa criticised the song choice, the production, the vocals, Gary said Louis had 'destroyed our night', and even Louis himself said the song choice wasn't great! It was only Nicole who made positive comments, and as she pointed out we'd performed as a four-piece for the very first time on live television.

GEORGE: I get very nervous speaking in front of famous people so when Dermot asked me to respond I just said we'd take all the comments on board and get better. But we were totally gutted.

JOSH: I was embarrassed after that opening night. Especially by my vocals. The other boys did really well but, personally, I was really disappointed in myself. I thought, *If that is our last performance and we go out, I will kick myself so hard for not doing as well as I could have done.* I was embarrassed for my friends and family. *What happened there?*

JJ: Then Sunday – the results day! I used to love Sundays before the *X Factor*, chilling with family at home, but now I hated Sundays! I never got really nervous before each week's performance but ahead of the results on Sundays I would absolutely crap myself. A bag of nerves. You are living in this amazing bubble and you don't want it to end but we knew this could easily end in Week 1 after those comments. So you can imagine how amazed and over the moon we all were when somehow they called our name out quite early and we were through!

GEORGE: We were so shocked when we got through! How could we get through with a song like that? We knew we had to work *so hard* to survive Week 2. We'd already learnt some helpful little techniques and tips you need to know about performing on a big stage and for TV, how to work the microphone, being aware of the cameras, that sort of thing. We now knew it was a lot about song choice as well.

That night after the show, we were getting a lot of hate on Twitter, which was hard to read. People were slagging us off as 1D wannabes. That was weird and something we hadn't expected. But we were through . . . somehow.

JOSH: We knew that for Week 2 we had to raise our game one hundred per cent, so the pressure was really on. I'd already moved the goalposts . . . again. Remember I was happy to get to Judges' Houses? Well, as soon as I got to Vegas I wanted to get to the live shows. Then as soon as we were singing live I wanted to go as far as we possibly could. I guess that's the competitive footballer in me!

GEORGE: WE SAT DOWN AND SAID, 'WHAT SORT OF MUSIC DO WE WANT TO DO? WHAT STYLING ARE WE COMFORTABLE WITH? WHAT IS UNION J ABOUT?'

BASICALLY WE HAD MORE INPUT THAT WEEK AND ASKED FOR SONGS THAT SHOWED OUR VOICES OFF MORE. JAYMI IS A MASSIVE POWER SINGER WITH A HUGE RANGE, JOSH HAS A WICKED R&B TONE, I'VE GOT A ROCKIER HUSKY TONE AND JJ HAS AN OPERATIC EDGE. WE HAVE ALL THESE DIFFERENT STYLES AND 'DON'T STOP ME NOW' DID NONE OF THEM JUSTICE.

JJ: Week 2 was a massive stepping stone. We wanted to get better and better and better. That first week was so bad but I'd say it was actually a blessing in disguise. We didn't want to drop to that level again. If we weren't in the studio singing we were in the Corinthia practising, getting our harmonies right. If there were no rooms free we'd be in the toilets, just rehearsing anywhere.

JAYMI: I was fighting so hard; we all were. We needed to do something. The production team were really backing us, but we needed to set our stall out ourselves, so we basically lived in the rehearsal studio sixteen hours a day. I was very keen to do

'Bleeding Love – remember Leona was my obsession! – because I felt it would give us an opportunity to showcase our vocals really well. Some of the boys wanted James Morrison's 'Broken Strings', and actually what happened was Kye Sones suggested that we do a mash-up of both. What a brilliant idea. I was so excited.

We worked damn hard. We worked our arses off from the minute we walked off stage Sunday night Week 1. We actually went straight to the producers and said, 'Something needs to change!' In our head it was like, *If we make a decision and we get it wrong at least it's our fault. No one else is to blame.* This is our career so only we can get it right.

JOSH: The producers had other song ideas but we put our foot down and they let us go with the mash-up, and my God it paid off massively.

JJ: The second week was still quite nerve-wracking, but we felt much more confident because we had rehearsed non-stop and we knew the songs sounded wicked. Everything about us from the first week to the next was so much better: the production, our clothing and most importantly our voices. It was an amazing transformation.

GEORGE: We were so much more confident. Everything was working, the vocals, the styling, the choreography. This was the moment we turned it round, massively! Tulisa was smiling so much as we performed. My dad was sitting in the crowd and I looked over at him and he was like, 'Yeah!' The atmosphere was amazing and the audience was amazing. Jaymi's incredible vocals were shining through.

JJ: We had to smash it. Everything about it was *us*. We felt like a band, not four individual solo artists.

JOSH: I thought it was one of our strongest performances: the transformation, how we looked, what we were wearing, the song choice, the vocals. All of a sudden we said to the other acts, 'We are here, hello! Maybe you should think of Union J as competition?!'

JJ: The judges' comments were fantastic! And we deserved that; every time we had bad comments we worked ten times harder the next week. But this was still early days, we were still getting to know each other's voices, so that was a massive turning point for us, a real confidence boost.

GEORGE: District3 – as GMD3 were now called – must have felt they had us beat in Week 1 and, to be fair, at that point they did. But after Week 2 things changed, and with that our rivalry stepped up a notch. That week District3 were in the bottom two with Melanie. We went straight through. Something had changed.

MALE
ARTISTES
DRESSING ROOM

think in a way that Week 2's performance was the start of Union J. It was *that* pivotal, that important. We had been ready and together at Judges Houses, but this was another level. It all came together in those two and a half minutes. I honestly think our careers were mapped out by that song, one hundred per cent.

 GEORGE: Then seven days later Week 3 was a bit of a lost week for us . . .

 JAYMI: Yes, it was pretty bland. A nothing week.

GEORGE: We did a Kelly Rowland track with some choreography but we felt a little awkward. We knew District3 were going to get a bounceback vote and we'd set our bar so high on the previous show, so we did feel pressure, but fortunately we got good comments and sailed through again. I was really pleased as the next show, Week 4, was Halloween week and because of my love for scary movies I really wanted to be there!

JOSH: We were starting to get into a weekly routine now, feeling like we understood how the show worked and how we had to operate as a band to get the best out of the situation. We slowly started to feel more comfortable and get into a rhythm. People started going home each week and the numbers were getting smaller and the hotel was getting less hectic.

Our routine would be: Monday, early-morning start, straight into practice where you try out – or 'routine' – a load of songs until something feels right. Sometimes we would routine thirty songs before we had the right choice. Within the week there'd be lots of PR and filming to do, like the James Bond premiere, we got to sing at Disneyland one week and there was always lots of filming for ITV2's *The Xtra Factor*, as well as footage for the main show and so on. You would head to the studio on Thursday and Friday for soundchecks and choreography, trying to polish everything.

Saturdays were always an early start: into a car, all contestants went to the studio in Wembley and had breakfast, then into hair, then make-up, perhaps a little sleep wherever you can because it gets so tiring over the course of a week, especially with all the nerves and adrenalin rushing round your body. More practice, then a last-minute soundcheck, go through it once, and friends and family could come in and see the full dress rehearsal. My mum came to every single show! The amount of times that people would step up Saturday night compared to their dress rehearsal, or you'd be shocked that on the live show they were actually nowhere near as good as in the week . . . You could never tell.

every week to work on. We were never complacent; we always had something to work on, to better ourselves with. You have to be able to accep and work with constructive criticism, and we did that.

GEORGE: So like I said, next up was Halloween Night and I was buzzing for it. I'd wanted to do something associated with *Twilight* because I knew our fans would be of an age where they were into all that, bu we ended up with Beyoncé's 'Sweet Dreams'. I was dressed up as a vampire which was really cool! This was actually one of my favourite weeks and thought this was our third week in a row where we smashed it. We all loved i and came off feeling confident, so we were really shocked to find ourselves in the bottom two.

JOSH: All week a few of us had thought we would be in the bottom two We are all worriers at times and we tend to feed off each other. There are always shock exits and when they said we were bottom two, I thought we were gone.

JAYMI: I was gutted. I was actually a little bit surprised because thought we did okay but something wasn't appealing to the viewers tha week because we were put up against Jade in the sing-off. She is amazing and beautiful and was one of our best friends, so that was difficult.

JJ: We wondered if our fans had thought we were safe that week and voted for District3 instead, because we were building a momentum and getting good comments, but District3 perhaps weren't evolving as much a that point. Our Survival Song was 'Perfect' by Pink and we did okay, but Jade smashed her performance.

JAYMI: It's tough singing for survival but, I've said this before, my boys are fighters. You have to be focused, in the zone. We had rehearsed the Survival Song all week as well as our main song so there were no excuses During the performance, I was trying to get my collar undone because it was too tight, so that was a little off-putting. But we weren't letting it go, it was a gritty performance. I did a massive ad-lib and afterwards some people said that was risky but I am not about playing safe. I love pulling it out of the bag, big notes are my thing. I knew I would riff at that point in the song, and why not?! I am confident and I know my limits. I was comfortable in the sing-off. I was fighting and I wasn't even overly nervous. It wasn't taking me over. I had control.

GEORGE: Survival Songs are always about the vocals, no production. Jade was quirky and cool and a great singer. But like Jaymi says, you can see the fight in our faces, we really wanted to win. Our body language tells you all you need to know about how much we wanted this. We bonded even more as a group in that sing-off. All you have in that moment is those three other guys. They are like your brothers, and you are standing shoulder to shoulder, fighting.

JOSH: Thank God that we got through the sing-off. Afterwards, my mum said, 'You looked defeated. If that happens again, don't look like that. Show more fight.' I watched it back and she was right! I looked like we'd already lost. The other three lads looked like they were fighting but I didn't. I sounded terrible. I couldn't look up. I've never been more nervous, shaking and struggling for breath and when I blew out I felt cold. Towards the end of the song I remember thinking, *This is it. This could be the last ever song for us. Give it everything!* That was a hard performance for me. So when we got the result on Sunday night and we were safely through I was ecstatic! I didn't want to be in the bottom two ever again . . .

JJ: Week 5 – the halfway point of the show. We knew we had to massively step it up after being in the bottom two the previous week. That had felt very negative. The public clearly weren't feeling something, so we had to change it around. When that happens you doubt yourself massively. It's a horrible feeling to think the public don't like you and that you are close to going home. We said to ourselves, *We have done something wrong, so what can we do to make it right?*

JAYMI: I didn't want to do the song choice, which was 'Love Story' by Taylor Swift. I will be completely honest and say we were difficult this week. We kicked off about everything, because we were so worried about being in the bottom two again. We'd been told that after being in the bottom two you come back and worry so much more and that was definitely the case. Everything felt wrong . . .

JJ: Like Jaymi says, we were doubting the song but everyone said we should go for it because it's for the girls, our fans . . .

JAYMI: Exactly. And thank God we listened to the professionals because I think this was our defining moment. This was, *Right, we are here! This is Union J!* (That song would become a crucial part of Union J's story after *X Factor* when we sang it on tour and at shows.) It was the first time since Week 1 that we had let someone else – namely the production team – decide our song for us.

GEORGE: You know you will get a bounceback vote the week after being in the bottom two, but we were still worried. We felt we needed a weapon at that point and we had been saving my guitar so that was how we changed it up for Week 5. All through the audition process I had sung with my guitar but then it got taken away from me for the live shows, so bringing it out again made it feel like a weapon and gave us more credibility, especially with lads who were watching on TV. We loved performing 'Love Story'. It was great. It was *us*, as ourselves.

JJ: The judges said it was our best performance so far and that we felt like a proper boy band. The performance had felt brilliant. We loved singing it and after hearing those comments we were hugging each other and having a laugh with it. Wicked.

JOSH: 'Love Story' was a really good week for us. Gary said it was a brilliant performance, Tulisa said we 'nailed it', Nicole loved it and Louis said, 'You could be the next big boy band!'

Every Sunday night, though, I was petrified. So scared, so nervous. I just kept thinking, *What if?* We kept progressing but we also kept getting in the bottom two. Sometimes with *X Factor*, getting positive comments isn't always a good thing because people think you are safe. When you get negative comments, such as in our first week, you get good voting. After the show had finished and they published the phone-vote statistics it turned out that in that catastrophic Week 1 we had actually come fourth, and yet we were the worst act on the night by far. But people felt sorry for us and knew we weren't safe, so they voted for us.

GEORGE: Layered harmonies were coming into it more, these three-piece harmonies. Every week we were getting better and better, because we were getting to know each other more and bonding. So Week 5 we went straight through, no problem. We had got our edge back and it felt amazing.

'**GEORGE:** LAYERED HARMONIES WERE COMING INTO IT MORE, THESE THREE-PIECE HARMONIES. EVERY WEEK WE WERE GETTING BETTER AND BETTER, BECAUSE WE WERE GETTING TO KNOW EACH OTHER MORE AND BONDING.'

11

OUR FINAL

JAYMI: Week 6 was an odd week in many ways but it also proved to be the single most important of the entire show for Union J. We were shattered by this point in the process, we were all exhausted and poorly, and we'd had weeks and weeks of sixteen-hour days, with no time off for a second – it was brilliant but it catches up on you.

GEORGE: We sang Coldplay's 'Fix You' and dedicated the performance to the Armed Forces. This was a special week for me because, as you now know, my brother is in the Marines, so I was really emotional. My guitar was there again and it felt like that was a part of us now. We looked better again as the styling was really cool, there were some great harmonies, we certainly sang better and I think all the emotions that we'd experienced from the sing-offs were now coming into each performance. We weren't just a blank canvas. This was my favourite week.

However, all day on the Sunday there was something weird in the air backstage. Everything felt really bizarre. We actually had a feeling we were in the bottom two, and so did District3. Behind the scenes there was an exclamation-mark sign everywhere, all these yellow hazard signs around the place, so everyone was saying, 'Is there gonna be a twist this week?' Something big was happening. When Dermot read out who was through it came down to us, District3 and Chris Maloney. We thought that was the twist, a triple sing-off. But then he put Chris through . . .

JJ: So this was the big moment for us: Union J versus District3. Who is going to be the top boy band? Game on. Obviously we had been up against them before and lost, but we felt much better about this sing-off because in such a short period of time, and purely by putting the work in, we had improved massively. They were still a wicked band, though, so this was gonna be a fight for our lives.

JOSH: Like JJ says, this was *the* week, because we simply had to beat District3. It was no use to us being the second-best boy band from *X Factor* . . . The stakes couldn't have been higher. It had all boiled down to this one sing-off.

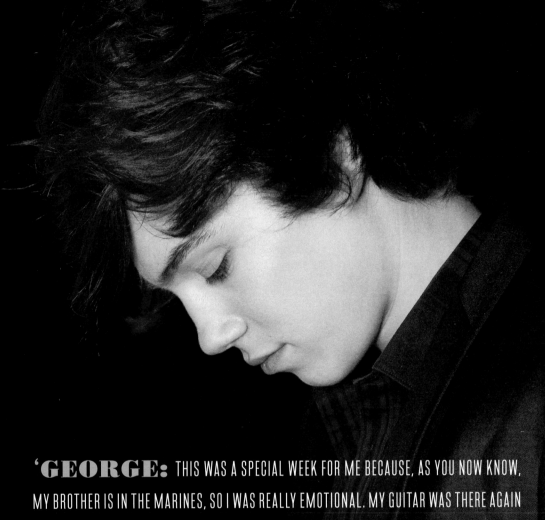

'**GEORGE:** THIS WAS A SPECIAL WEEK FOR ME BECAUSE, AS YOU NOW KNOW, MY BROTHER IS IN THE MARINES, SO I WAS REALLY EMOTIONAL. MY GUITAR WAS THERE AGAIN AND IT FELT LIKE THAT WAS A PART OF US NOW.'

JAYMI: When I heard we were in the bottom two against District3, I have never been more determined in my entire life to win. I was so focused, I was like, *It won't happen. I am not gonna let this happen. It is not up for debate. I am not even putting it out there.* We knew that whoever won would then get the entire boy-band vote and that would be a massive boost in later weeks. I was more concerned about being the last boy band standing in the competition – in terms of our career and our futures, that was more important than getting to the final.

JJ: I remember backstage before the sing-off we were psyching ourselves up by punching each other and getting really wound up. It was like going out to a big football game or a boxing match. We were literally fighting for survival.

JOSH: That was exactly how it felt! It was a fight. This was everything, our career . . . the single most important performance we have ever done, one hundred per cent. There was no option to lose, no way we could lose, that was how we had to think. My whole attitude had changed from the first sing-off. There was no more defeatism. I was like, *Come on! Let's do this!*

'**JJ:** I REMEMBER BACKSTAGE BEFORE THE SING-OFF WE WERE PSYCHING OURSELVES UP BY PUNCHING EACH OTHER AND GETTING REALLY WOUND UP. IT WAS LIKE GOING OUT TO A BIG FOOTBALL GAME OR A BOXING MATCH. WE WERE LITERALLY FIGHTING FOR SURVIVAL.'

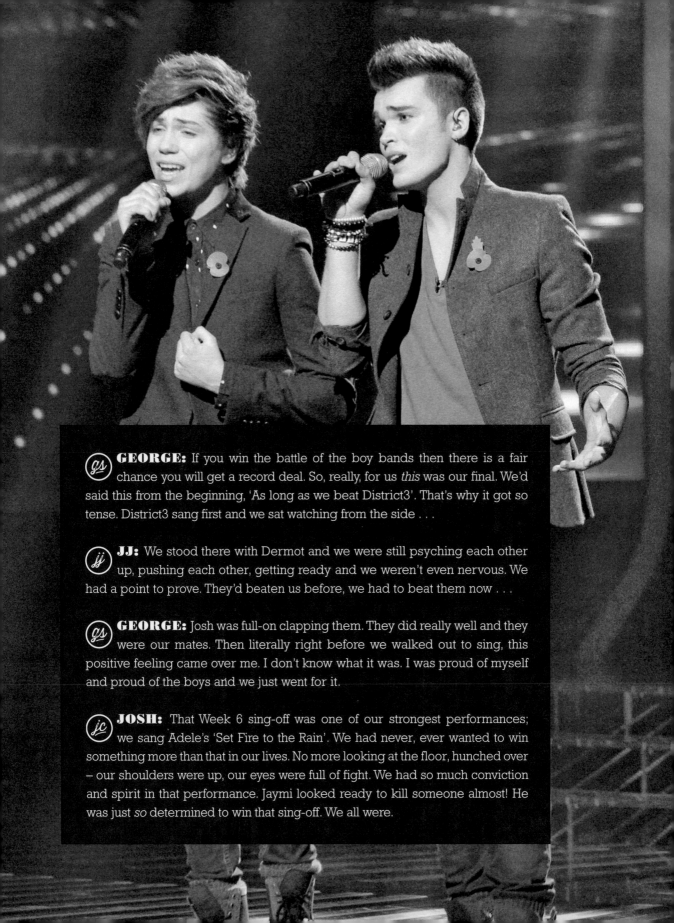

GEORGE: If you win the battle of the boy bands then there is a fair chance you will get a record deal. So, really, for us *this* was our final. We'd said this from the beginning, 'As long as we beat District3'. That's why it got so tense. District3 sang first and we sat watching from the side . . .

JJ: We stood there with Dermot and we were still psyching each other up, pushing each other, getting ready and we weren't even nervous. We had a point to prove. They'd beaten us before, we had to beat them now . . .

GEORGE: Josh was full-on clapping them. They did really well and they were our mates. Then literally right before we walked out to sing, this positive feeling came over me. I don't know what it was. I was proud of myself and proud of the boys and we just went for it.

JOSH: That Week 6 sing-off was one of our strongest performances; we sang Adele's 'Set Fire to the Rain'. We had never, ever wanted to win something more than that in our lives. No more looking at the floor, hunched over – our shoulders were up, our eyes were full of fight. We had so much conviction and spirit in that performance. Jaymi looked ready to kill someone almost! He was just *so* determined to win that sing-off. We all were.

'DO YOU KNOW WHERE WE GOT THAT AMAZING WILL TO WIN FROM? THAT MOMENT WHEN THEY KICKED US OFF AT

BOOTCAMP.

EVEN AMONG ALL THOSE SAD FEELINGS BACK THEN AND THE RESIGNATION THAT IT SEEMED TO BE OVER, I REMEMBER LOVING MY BOYS IN THE BAND SO MUCH AT THAT MOMENT THAT BOOTCAMP REJECTION HAD BONDED US SO MUCH. AND GEORGE HAD EXPERIENCED THE VERY SAME SHATTERING DISAPPOINTMENT, SO WE WERE ALL IN THIS TOGETHER. IN FACT, **I'D GO AS FAR AS TO SAY THAT THAT MOMENT IN BOOTCAMP WAS THE REASON WHY WE WOULD LATER GO ON TO THE SEMI-FINALS OF X FACTOR. BECAUSE IT HAD BEEN TAKEN AWAY FROM US ONCE BEFORE AND THERE WAS ABSOLUTELY NO WAY THAT THAT WAS EVER GOING TO BE ALLOWED TO HAPPEN AGAIN.** WE WERE GOING TO WIN, THERE WAS NO DOUBT IN MY MIND. IF IT EVER CAME DOWN TO A SING-OFF AGAIN – WHICH I KNEW IT WOULD BECAUSE THAT'S THE WAY FATE WORKS – THEN WE WERE GOING TO WIN. NOTHING WAS GOING TO STOP US. WE HAD GOT BATTERED, BUT IT MAKES YOU STRONGER. IT MADE ME STRONGER. IT MADE US STRONGER. WE WERE GOING TO WIN THIS TIME. WE HAD TO. END OF

JJ: Everyone had been a little bit concerned by our song choice because obviously doing an Adele song is a big ask! But we sang it well and we felt confident. We were happy with that performance.

JAYMI: I had lost weight; I didn't eat that well during the whole show. Just with being busy and so tired all the time. I love the jacket I wore that week. I still have it!

Seriously, though, we were fighting. Our career was hanging in the balance. We were a unit. Like a tank, a bulldozer, the four of us were unstoppable in that sing-off; there's something about the four of us when we are put in situations like that with our backs to the wall. We will take down anything that gets in our way.

GEORGE: This was a turning point in our careers and our lives, and we had to do everything to get through. We had become brothers now. We were not just members of a boy band; there was an emotional connection. The song was perfect, and all the harmonies were a step up. We had done these lovely romantic songs and fun boy-band songs too, but it shocked the judges when we sang this really big song and started harmonising. The fighting spirit in that performance was kinda like putting our middle finger up to people who had doubted us.

JAYMI: It was a great survival performance . . . I thought we'd done enough.

JOSH: Louis completely had our backs. He pulled out everything he could to get us through each week. When it came to the judges' decisions, he refused to choose an act to send home. Both bands knew he would do that. He was a great mentor. He really cared and you can see how emotional he was; we got really close to Louis.

GEORGE: WE COULD HEAR THE CROWD CHANTING 'UNION J! UNION J!' IN THE BACKGROUND, AND OBVIOUSLY THE JUDGES COULD HEAR THAT TOO, SO WE WERE LIKE, **PLEASE LISTEN TO THEM!** I THINK IT IS FAIR TO SAY THAT WE HAD MORE OF A CONNECTION WITH LOUIS, MORE OF A RELATIONSHIP. WE USED TO GO TO HIS DRESSING ROOM AND HAVE CHATS WITH HIM, BUT DISTRICT3 NEVER DID, SO IN ONE WAY WE THOUGHT HE MIGHT VOTE TO SAVE US, BUT HE IS A LOYAL AND VERY FAIR MENTOR AND HE WOULDN'T CHOOSE.

JJ: So Louis wouldn't judge it, but even then we honestly didn't know which way it would go. Gary said that he thought District3 had had a bad week, and he was surprised because he'd previously seen them as the boy band that was outperforming their rivals. He said we looked like we 'wanted it' more and so he voted for us to go through. So now it was Nicole's turn . . . and when she started talking to District3, I could sense she was going to save us. When she sent District3 home by voting to save us it was the best feeling ever! Sheer elation!

JAYMI: When Nicole saved us over District3 it was the best feeling. As much as I love District3 it felt really good to win. Now we were the last band standing . . . which is what we had wanted all along. Every week we had been compared to them. Right back in bootcamp when they had paired us off against each other all the time, through Judges' Houses and then the live shows, we felt like we were never seen for who we were away from that 'rivalry', but now we could be solely judged on our own merits. I had a few beers that night. I maybe got a little bit merry!

JOSH: I was so happy to win against District3, I know that probably sounds really bad, but this was everything that we wanted. The pressure just instantly lifted. Suddenly we were the most successful group in the competition. After One Direction had become so huge having been third, we kinda thought we didn't necessarily need to win the whole show. But we did need to win the battle of the boy bands. For the next two weeks after that, we were so strong. The pressure was off, so we could go out there and just perform, as opposed to getting worked up and stressed about each week.

GEORGE: Josh is right. I think it's fair to say that winning *X Factor* wasn't our competition. It was about being the best boy band, as well as the last band in the show. And we had done it. We were really proud of Union J as a team, this band of brothers that we had become, so now it was about seeing how far we could go, but mainly about just enjoying ourselves from here onwards.

JAYMI: First thing the next morning we were in rehearsals early! That's Union J all over: no let up, keep on pushing. But, yes, it did feel different. We had achieved our goal and the pressure was totally off. We went to Disney and sang 'Call Me Maybe' there, which was a once-in-a-lifetime experience, and there were also all these whispers and rumours that we might get offered a major-label record deal. What a week! I was loving my life!

JOSH: It's funny, because I kept moving the goalposts. That football brain of mine just kept raising expectations. I totally agree with the boys about beating District3, that was absolutely our main aim. But as soon as we had done that I found myself thinking, *Hey, maybe we could get to the final . . . and if we get to the final, then maybe . . .*

JJ: Week 7 was a pretty simple week. We sang 'Call Me Maybe' and got voted through. There was probably an element of bounceback voting, plus we were all very relaxed and enjoying ourselves, so it was a great energetic, happy performance.

'**JOSH:** I WAS SO HAPPY TO WIN AGAINST DISTRICT3, I KNOW THAT PROBABLY SOUNDS REALLY BAD, BUT THIS WAS EVERYTHING THAT WE WANTED. THE PRESSURE JUST INSTANTLY LIFTED. SUDDENLY WE WERE THE MOST SUCCESSFUL GROUP IN THE COMPETITION.'

12

STANDING OUT FROM THE CROWD

JAYMI: Week 8 was a big week for me personally, because I decided to come out publicly in the media. I just wanted to enjoy the process of the show, to enjoy every single step without anything being hidden. I am all about people being open and I had been out since I was fourteen. As you now know I told my parents at a young age, and I think, looking back, that's what made me so strong, despite all the knock-backs I suffered, because I was comfortable with who I was.

I love my gay life and all the friends I've made from the gay scene. That bar that I told you about, where I collected glasses when I was fifteen, I used to go in there with fake ID and they said, 'You can't keep doing this!', so they offered me a proper job instead. I made a family there. I have got brothers and sisters and dads and mums on the gay scene.

Being on *X Factor* is the best thing that's ever happened to me professionally, but the best thing in my life is being gay and being comfortable with who I am and loving that and having a loving relationship with Olly. I met Olly nearly four years ago in a bar in Luton. I'd pretty much resigned myself to not having a relationship, as some of my exes hadn't turned out to be 'Prince Charming'. But on this particular night I had been out with friends and we'd turned up to a new club that had opened. I remember the first time I saw Olly working behind the bar, thinking how gorgeous he was. We hit it off straight away and have literally been inseparable since. I knew straight away he was 'The One' and I have never been happier. We have spent the most amazing four years together and have grown stronger every day. He has been a massive support to me, encouraging me to pursue my dream even if it meant we didn't have any money. He has been so selfless and supportive during this process and only wants me to be happy. I know I am extremely lucky to have found someone who understands me on every level; I never really believed in soul-mates before, but I have found mine and count myself the luckiest guy in the world to have him.

Being gay gave me something else to fight for, it clearly made me stronger. I wanted to fight for who I am. If I have got a cause to fight for, there's no telling me that I can't do something. I am so passionate and proud about where I am coming from, I couldn't be more proud of being gay.

There's also a very important point to be made about my coming out during *X Factor*. A very dear friend of mine, a drag queen called Betty Buss, used to tell me so many stories about when he was younger and going to gay clubs. About how you used to knock on doors, then a little hatch would open and you'd say a password to get in, and then at the end of the night you'd have to check to make sure no one was there before you ran to your car. Those stories are important because those people fought for my generation. They stood up for themselves and for future generations of the gay community; they made attitudes change. Now it's legal for gay people to get married in a church. This is manic stuff that has changed in my lifetime! They fought for me, for my gay life, and they fought for what was important to them – and we can never forget that or take it for granted.

So with regards to coming out during *X Factor,* it was quite a simple decision for me. People said I was 'brave' and all that, but I just didn't wanna hide. It's all about educating people. There is still a stigma attached to being gay in certain circles. For example, some people think it is a promiscuous lifestyle, while some narrow-minded people think it is not 'the norm', that it's not what people are taught about, it's not the 'convention'. My family are so well educated and are completely happy that my male friend dresses up as a woman. They see that as a perfectly normal lifestyle. That is no different to going out in fancy dress. That is just a way of expressing himself. You can be black, white, disabled, young or old – there's a place for you in the gay scene. It might be hard to come out to your family or friends and they might not accept it, but there's somewhere you belong. That is why I was so passionate about coming out publicly in Week 8

because I knew there would be kids thinking, *I can't come out because my dad won't accept it. I am like, Screw your dad! If he doesn't accept it, he has to get used to the fact. It's who you are!*

Initially I didn't want to do it on the show because I didn't want critics to suggest I was using it for votes. I wanted to be judged solely on our singing. But my saving grace was Rylan, because he was openly gay, very flamboyant and proud. Lucy, Jade and Charlie from MK1 were also all openly gay so I knew my news wasn't going to be this massive shock *X Factor* announcement.

Specifically, that week was about being yourself, and everyone in my life outside the show knew I was gay. I had a boyfriend I adored, so why shouldn't I tell people? I really hoped it would help someone out there. The boys in the band were brilliant, so supportive. We actually laughed about it, you know, 'Every boy band has to have a gay member!'

I love my boys, there is something so special about us, I love us to bits; to think at school I was that stereotypical fat gay kid who wore glasses! But I came from that to being in one of the best boy bands ever!

I don't see it as a brave decision, but it was a very important thing for me to do. I am going to succeed in life and I want to be proof that you can be gay and you can do something with your life. You can be the fat gay kid at school and still live the most amazing life. If I help one kid then that's enough, It was worth it. It was the best thing I ever did.

GEORGE: By Week 8, we'd run out of song ideas, so we went back to our first choice for Week 1, which was 'The Winner Takes It All', along with 'I'll Be There' by The Jackson 5.

JAYMI: After the ABBA song the comments were brilliant! Nicole said, 'Jaymi, I am proud of you for being courageous and strong this week, my love.' That was really kind of her to acknowledge what had happened in my private life. Very classy. Gary said, 'I feel so good about this band,' and then stated that we were 'on a roll'.

JJ: Then we sang the Jackson 5 song and we had yet more amazing comments. Tulisa said it was our best night in the entire show, Nicole loved it too, although Gary was a little negative. So we came off feeling great, but we were gutted to find ourselves in the bottom two once more, up against Rylan this time.

I thought we did two great performances and we all really thoroughly enjoyed every minute, but we were in the bottom two again!

JAYMI: Yes, but that was sod's law because there were only five of us left by now – even James was in the bottom two the previous week.

JJ: Fair point. This time the sing-off – the very last sing-off in the series – was against Rylan. He was wicked. He'd kept getting so many negative comments over the various weeks but he never let it affect him and we loved him. His performances were always top-notch. Every week I would think, *I can't wait to see Rylan.* He is one of the nicest guys I've ever met, genuinely. I will always keep in touch with him and no one has got a bad word to say about him. To go up against him was gutting, but he said to us, 'I am ready to go. It is time.' He is an absolute star.

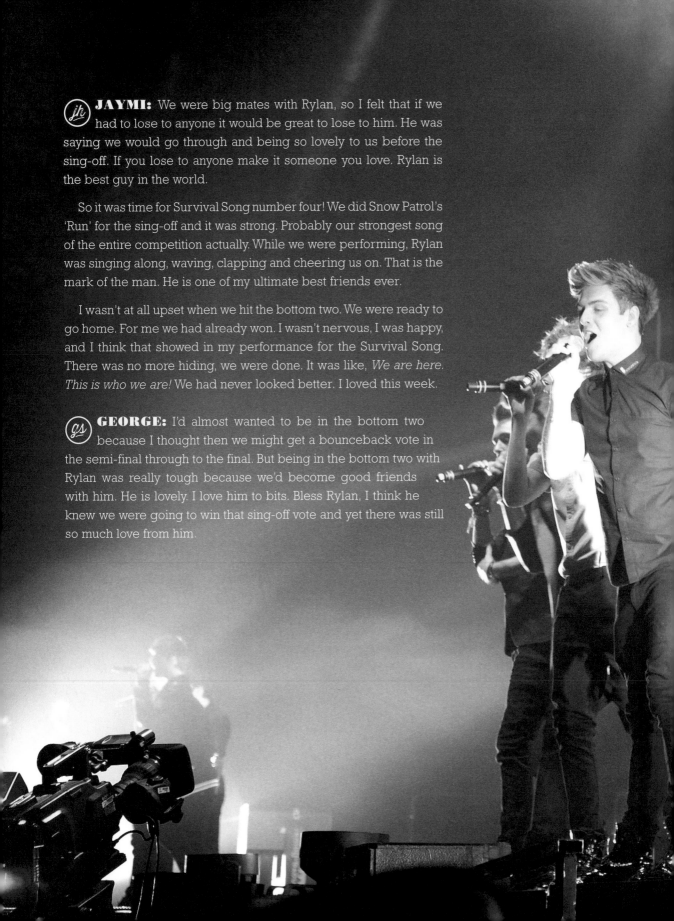

JAYMI: We were big mates with Rylan, so I felt that if we had to lose to anyone it would be great to lose to him. He was saying we would go through and being so lovely to us before the sing-off. If you lose to anyone make it someone you love. Rylan is the best guy in the world.

So it was time for Survival Song number four! We did Snow Patrol's 'Run' for the sing-off and it was strong. Probably our strongest song of the entire competition actually. While we were performing, Rylan was singing along, waving, clapping and cheering us on. That is the mark of the man. He is one of my ultimate best friends ever.

I wasn't at all upset when we hit the bottom two. We were ready to go home. For me we had already won. I wasn't nervous, I was happy, and I think that showed in my performance for the Survival Song. There was no more hiding, we were done. It was like, *We are here. This is who we are!* We had never looked better. I loved this week.

GEORGE: I'd almost wanted to be in the bottom two because I thought then we might get a bounceback vote in the semi-final through to the final. But being in the bottom two with Rylan was really tough because we'd become good friends with him. He is lovely. I love him to bits. Bless Rylan, I think he knew we were going to win that sing-off vote and yet there was still so much love from him.

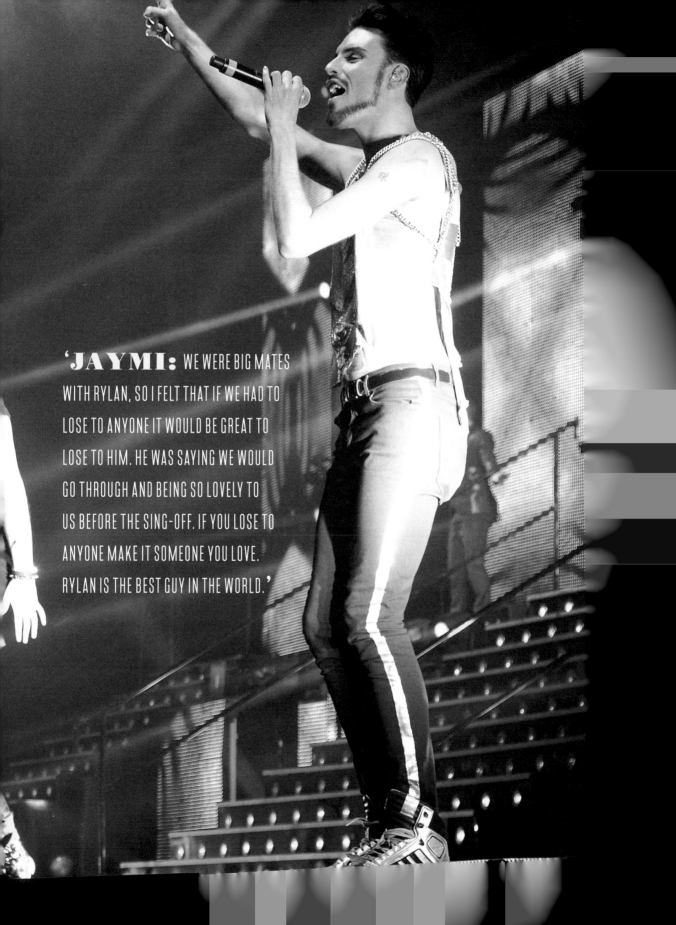

'JAYMI: WE WERE BIG MATES WITH RYLAN, SO I FELT THAT IF WE HAD TO LOSE TO ANYONE IT WOULD BE GREAT TO LOSE TO HIM. HE WAS SAYING WE WOULD GO THROUGH AND BEING SO LOVELY TO US BEFORE THE SING-OFF. IF YOU LOSE TO ANYONE MAKE IT SOMEONE YOU LOVE. RYLAN IS THE BEST GUY IN THE WORLD.'

JAYMI: After the sing-off Gary Barlow said, 'You are the band everyone is going to want to sign.' We couldn't believe what he was saying. We got really strong comments, even from Rylan's mentor Nicole, bless her. When Dermot said we were through and Rylan was going home, I just went straight over to Rylan and gave him a massive hug. I was so sad to see him go but we were both happy for each other. He is one of a kind. I love the bones of him.

JJ: I really felt the benefit of being in a group by this stage. Gradually all these acts had been leaving and the mood backstage and at the hotel was changing. Some nights – such as when Ella went out in a shock exit – the mood in the *X Factor* camp was really depressed and weird. But being a band we always had each other to cheer ourselves up, to make someone laugh or just chat stuff through. I genuinely felt for the solo artists, because although they made friends with other contestants they were still on their own, alone with their thoughts. That must have been tough. I was loving being with my boys! So here we were, Week 9 – bring it on!

JAYMI: From day one of *X Factor* I'd said to the boys I thought we'd come out fourth. I just had a gut feeling. And now that we were the last band left, that was already job done.

JOSH: Ha ha! If I am totally honest, at that point I was thinking, *How incredible would it be to get to the final?!* Week 9 was my favourite performance. We sang 'Beneath Your Beautiful' by Emeli Sandé and Labrinth, which is a great tune. I wanted to take it all in. I tend to do this with any big experience, even holidays, for example. When I know something is coming to the end I really soak it all in.

And this was a big song for me. I had a lot of tough vocals to get right. We looked like a group, and I think that was our best performance on a Saturday. We did two songs and the comments were incredible. We'd done everything we could, so we were happy with whatever happened.

GEORGE: Our last song was 'Already There' and if you listen to the lyrics, they felt so relevant to our situation, even if we came fourth and didn't make the final, there was that feeling that we were indeed 'already there'. There were all these rumours of record deals and a lot of music-industry interest in us, so there was that sense that perhaps the result didn't matter. It felt like a farewell song to me. It was a proud moment for Union J.

JAYMI: You're right, this was a strong week for us. Josh and the team picked this song. Like George says, it did feel like a farewell song. And we were knackered, burnt out.

JJ: I found that semi-final Sunday really hard. It was absolutely horrid. I wanted to get to the final, I don't mind saying that. We thought we had proved ourselves. We were the last band standing, and our last performances were great, but surely everyone wants to be in the final? Gary Barlow kept saying the record labels were going to be fighting over us, which was great to hear, but there are plenty of bands that have been in the *X Factor* semi-finals and you've never heard of them again.

JOSH: I remember looking across the stage in the first week when Dermot was revealing the result and there was this long line of people, but now there was hardly anyone left on that stage.

JOSH: Out of all the boys backstage I got really close to Jahméne and James. I had a lot in common with James in terms of football, and we also got on great with Jahméne – those boys were like our brothers. I wanted Jahméne to get through almost as much as us, for both of them to get through, in fact. After James went I whispered to George, 'We are going home.' I would have loved for it to be a Union J, James and Jahméne final, it would have been so perfect. So when Chris went through to the final and it was either us or Jahméne going home, I was really disappointed. Then when Dermot put Jahméne through to the final, I was so happy for him, but I was gutted for us too. We later found out that we had lost out to Chris by just 0.6 per cent of the votes.

GEORGE: When they said we were going home, yes, I was gutted, but at the same time the bubble had already burst. Ella had gone, she was like our little sister, and Rylan had gone. We felt we'd done enough to kickstart a career and so it was an odd feeling of calm really.

JAYMI: I wasn't sad at all when we were knocked out, genuinely. We were ready. Just look at our faces when Dermot is revealing the result. It was time. Louis knew we were going; we all knew. That was it, over.

We all went home to the hotel that night but we had *Daybreak* the next morning, which was a git because it meant we were up at five in the morning! I slept really well for the first time in months. My head hit the pillow and I was out like a light. For the last three weeks we had all been dead on our arses.

GEORGE:

THE MORNING AFTER THE

X FACTOR

FINAL IS A REALLY STRANGE DAY BECAUSE YOU ARE SUDDENLY OUT OF THIS BUBBLE THAT YOU HAVE LIVED IN FOR MONTHS, THEN BANG! IT'S BACK TO REALITY.

AND ON THAT MORNING I HAD A MASSIVE DEMONSTRATION OF MY POST-**X FACTOR** REALITY. I GOT MY AUNTY LISA TO PICK ME UP WITH BRAD AND BRON. IT WAS THE FIRST TIME I'D PROPERLY SEEN THEM FOR AGES . . . BUT THE CAR GOT MOBBED! THIS WAS MY FIRST TIME OUTSIDE **X FACTOR** WITH MY FAMILY AND TO EXPERIENCE WHAT MY NEW LIFE WOULD BE LIKE WAS A BIG SHOCK. WE WERE IN THIS CAR PARK AND AS SOON AS THE SHUTTER ROLLED UP AND WE STARTED TO DRIVE OUT WE SAW HUNDREDS OF FANS OUTSIDE RUSHING TOWARDS US. I WAS IN THE FRONT SEAT AND THEY ACTUALLY FORCED THE SHUTTER UP OUT OF THE WAY AND SWARMED ROUND THE CAR. FANS WERE BANGING ON THE WINDOWS, GIRLS WERE CRYING AND THROWING NOTES TO ME, AND THEY WERE SHOUTING, 'SORRY WE DIDN'T VOTE FOR YOU ENOUGH!' I KNEW THEN THAT MY LIFE HAD COMPLETELY CHANGED.

JJ: The first morning after our exit was sad, of course, but I wasn't too bad. I was happy to go back to see my family and my friends (after some interviews!). I was craving a bit of normality. Everyone in Newmarket had supported me so brilliantly, I was really touched. It's only a small horse-racing town and they had all come together and backed me massively, and I will always be grateful for that. Everyone in racing and at John Godstone's and Michael Stoute's where I worked has been so supportive. I love going back there when I've got time off, riding out again and catching up with friends and family, basically getting back to my old ways!

JAYMI: THE MONDAY MORNING WAS SO EXCITING, WOW! THE REST OF OUR LIVES ARE JUST STARTING. I WAS SO EXCITED, BUZZING, VERY HAPPY. AND WE WERE GOING BACK TO PERFORM AT THE FINAL BUT UNDER NO PRESSURE - IT WAS JUST A BRILLIANT WEEK. WE NEVER MISSED A WEEK OF X FACTOR. WE DID THE WHOLE SHOW FROM START TO FINISH AND I AM IMMENSELY PROUD OF THAT.

JJ: My little sister Otea is quite a shy girl and after I came off the show I found out she'd had a lot of attention from her friends at school! One day soon after she told me her headmaster wanted to speak to me and he said that every morning in assembly Otea would stand up and talk about *X Factor* and tell everyone what had been happening. That really touched me, it brought a tear to my eye.

GEORGE: The Corinthia hotel had been our home for nearly three months and that was all over too. Everyone was going to be moving out and heading for the final in Manchester. I was actually glad that we had that week off to go home, catch up with friends and family, relax, sleep, eat well and just enjoy ourselves without any stress or pressure.

Our families came to help us unpack from the Corinthia. You can imagine how many things we'd bought and how many freebies we'd been given in those three months! It felt like moving home; it was really emotional. We went into Jaymi's room and Josh just burst out crying. It was the end of a journey but the start of a new one, and all four of us hugged for ages, crying. We were so proud of each other.

The final was a completely different vibe, and to be fair we might not have enjoyed that night as much if we'd actually been competing. As it was, we just went along and really enjoyed the night.

JOSH: We loved every minute of *X Factor*. Part of me wishes that I had taken it all in a bit more. I actually wish I could do it again! There's no better feeling than going out there on a Saturday night, looking down that lens with the red light and knowing there are ten million people watching. What a privilege!

We had the week off and chilled, and it was amazing to see my family and friends again after being cocooned away so long. I will be honest, though, and say that I found it hard being at the final but not as a contestant, because I still wanted to win the show; the other boys were a lot better about it and really enjoyed themselves, but I was gutted I wasn't there competing, and that I wasn't up on that stage with Jahméne and James. Don't get me wrong, it was good fun to perform and do that group song, but I would still have liked to have seen my dream three in the final.

JJ: We enjoyed the final but already our minds were else-where. We wanted to have a career after the show as Union J. This was about much more than just *X Factor* now. We would do anything for a record deal and there was all this talk of these labels being after our signatures. And we were ready for the challenge. As soon as we came out of the show we were focused again immediately: Right, what is next? What do we need to do next?

13

OUR NEW REALITY

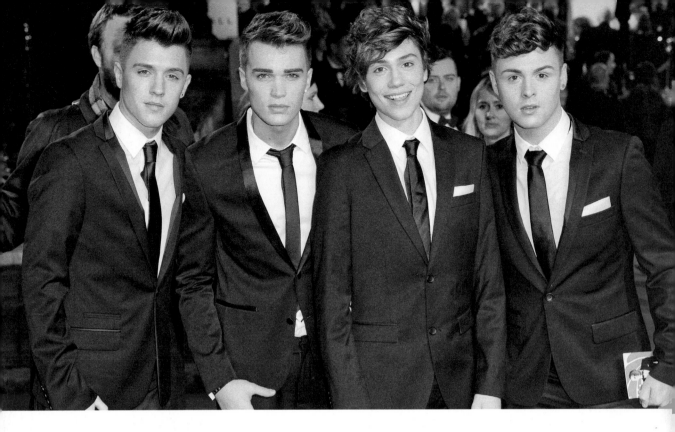

JAYMI: In the days and weeks after *X Factor*, we had loads of live appearances, TV and press to do, so we were still very busy, but we didn't have the same pressure on us. I felt like we could enjoy ourselves more. And obviously there was such a buzz every day! Like George said earlier, we were very shocked by the reaction of the fans. We loved it, of course, but I'm not sure the police did! We had to have police escorts at airports, and at gigs the fans were crazy!

JOSH: The gigs we have done so far have just been incredible! People are there solely to see Union J and the energy and excitement is overwhelming. We are so excited to think that this is what we can do every day of our lives! The screaming whenever we walk out is just deafening. That mad fan reaction was a big shock to us – we had heard that people were into us and, of course, we could see Twitter comments and all that, but until we actually went out there and started gigging we didn't realise the scale of that fan interest. We had been protected from that by the *X Factor* bubble, so when we first witnessed this mayhem it was the most amazing feeling. Mind you, I didn't enjoy being away from my beautiful cat Oreo again! Ha ha!

'**JOSH:** THE GIGS WE HAVE DONE SO FAR HAVE JUST BEEN INCREDIBLE! PEOPLE ARE THERE SOLELY TO SEE UNION J AND THE ENERGY AND EXCITEMENT IS OVERWHELMING.'

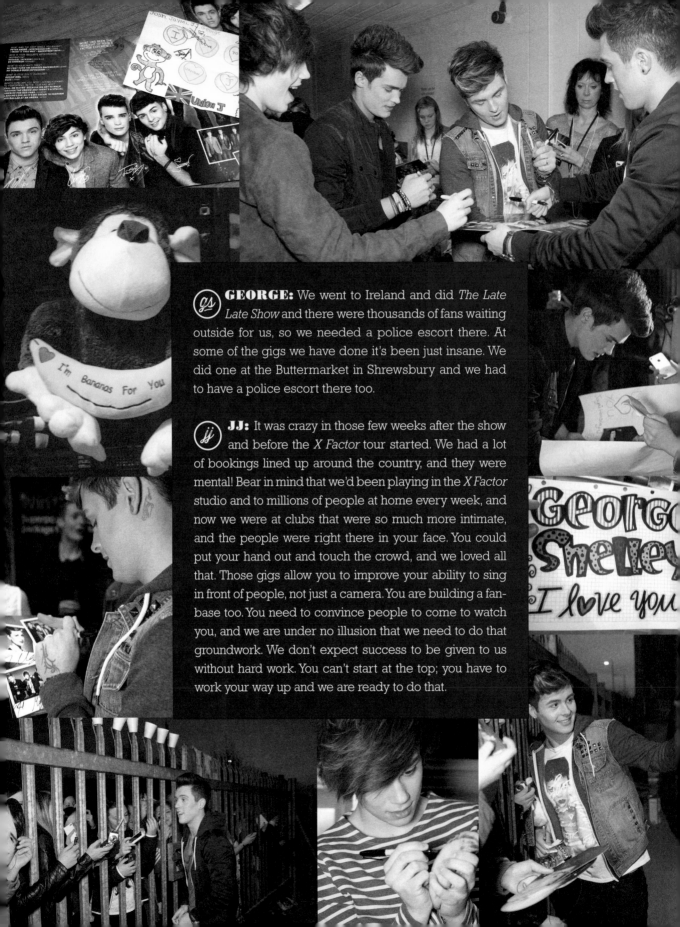

GEORGE: We went to Ireland and did *The Late Late Show* and there were thousands of fans waiting outside for us, so we needed a police escort there. At some of the gigs we have done it's been just insane. We did one at the Buttermarket in Shrewsbury and we had to have a police escort there too.

JJ: It was crazy in those few weeks after the show and before the *X Factor* tour started. We had a lot of bookings lined up around the country, and they were mental! Bear in mind that we'd been playing in the *X Factor* studio and to millions of people at home every week, and now we were at clubs that were so much more intimate, and the people were right there in your face. You could put your hand out and touch the crowd, and we loved all that. Those gigs allow you to improve your ability to sing in front of people, not just a camera. You are building a fan-base too. You need to convince people to come to watch you, and we are under no illusion that we need to do that groundwork. We don't expect success to be given to us without hard work. You can't start at the top; you have to work your way up and we are ready to do that.

'JOSH: THAT'S ONE OF THE MANY WEIRD THINGS ABOUT **X FACTOR:** YOU GO FROM BEING COMPLETELY UNKNOWN AT 7 P.M. ON THE FIRST SATURDAY TO TEN MILLION PEOPLE KNOWING WHO YOU ARE AN HOUR OR SO LATER. '

JOSH: It wasn't until we left the show that we realised the extent of the fans' interest in us. That's one of the many weird things about *X Factor:* you go from being completely unknown at 7 p.m. on the first Saturday to ten million people knowing who you are an hour or so later. That's why a lot of contestants go crazy. It is such an overnight change and there's no instruction manual for how to handle it. At first I just found it weird. Why would people be interested in Josh from Camberley, who likes his football and music? In my boring life?

Loads of fans write us letters and I read them as much as possible; one girl gave me a letter when we did that Shrewsbury gig. She'd had some pretty sad stuff happen to her and she said that I had helped her become stronger and cope with life. For us that's an incredible feeling to think that what you are doing is making a difference, making other people smile, and that is the single best motivation. The success is brilliant, of course it is, and maybe a bit of money too, but to get letters like that is really moving and makes you feel very lucky.

JAYMI: While we were doing these gigs and all the PR behind the scenes we were talking to record labels about a deal, which for all of us was a dream come true. During the latter stages of the show we had heard rumours about labels being after us, but I knew from my many painful experiences that until the ink is dry on the contract anything can go wrong! Thankfully there was a lot of interest in us and eventually we decided to go with RCA! Wow!

JJ: We never dreamed that we'd sign with a label like RCA. They've got acts like Justin Timberlake, Britney Spears, Pink, Beyoncé, Chris Broon, Christina Aguilera, and Ke$ha to name but a few – and also such a history! That happened really quickly, and within a very short space of time the contracts were signed, which was just the ultimate dream for all of us.

Luck was on our side but we have worked really hard for this. Without wanting to sound cheesy, without the support of people throughout *X Factor* we wouldn't have got that record deal. So I'd like to say a massive thank you to everyone who voted for us. You made our dreams come alive.

'JJ: WE NEVER DREAMED THAT WE'D SIGN WITH A LABEL LIKE RCA. THEY'VE GOT ACTS LIKE BRITNEY, CHRISTINA, FOO FIGHTERS AND KINGS OF LEON TO NAME BUT A FEW – AND ALSO SUCH A HISTORY! THAT HAPPENED REALLY QUICKLY AND WITHIN A VERY SHORT SPACE OF TIME THE CONTRACTS WERE SIGNED, WHICH WAS JUST THE ULTIMATE DREAM FOR ALL OF US.'

JAYMI: Then in late January it was back out on the road for the *X Factor* tour. At times that was hard work, but it was great to see all our friends again. When that tour ended it was sad because we didn't know when we would see some of them again, but then people like Rylan I am in touch with constantly. District3 too, I love those boys. Ella, Jahméne, loads of them.

JOSH: When the tour finished I was really sad. I am the type of person who gets attached to people quickly. I need people around me all the time otherwise I feel very lonely and I felt like this tour was another family. So it was a very emotional time for me on the final day.

GEORGE: Being completely honest, I didn't enjoy the tour as much as I enjoyed the show! We were with District3 a lot of the time on tour, which was quite awkward, and certain people were swanning around as if they had won the show. A couple of people had changed in the gap between the final and the tour, which was quite odd. But it was great to see old friends and hear all their exciting news!

We had started work on our debut single – which we will tell you about later – by the time of the *X Factor* tour, we'd had scores of photo shoots, done a video shoot for the debut single – all these exciting things were happening, and then we went on tour for a few weeks. Crazy! Shortly after, when it came to designing Union J's logo, I submitted my own ideas to the record label to be considered with all the work by the other graphic designers they normally use, and they chose mine! So that was really exciting!

We are just so excited to get our debut album out, and see what the fans make of our music. The fans are incredible. They have seen our whole journey and they themselves have been a major part of that journey. That's why they are so connected to us, they played a massive role in us being successful. They saw us evolve from this crappy boy band singing an awful cover of Queen into an act that made it all the way to Week 9 . . . and beyond. And let's not forget they voted for us every week . . . and without that where would we be?

GEORGE:

'THEN IN LATE JANUARY IT WAS BACK OUT ON THE ROAD FOR THE **X FACTOR TOUR.**

AT TIMES THAT WAS HARD WORK, BUT IT WAS GREAT TO SEE ALL OUR FRIENDS AGAIN.'

'**JJ :** I WOULD SAY TO ANYONE WHO IS THINKING OF DOING **X FACTOR** IT IS THE MOST AMAZING EXPERIENCE!'

OUR NEW ALBUM

GEORGE: JAYMI MENTIONED EARLIER ABOUT GOING INTO THE STUDIO TO RECORD OUR FIRST SINGLE; WELL, OF COURSE YOU ALL KNOW NOW THAT IT WAS CALLED

'CARRY YOU'

WHICH WE RELEASED IN THE FIRST WEEK OF JUNE 2013.

JOSH: Actually, we started work in the studio way back, even before the *X Factor* tour. 'Carry You' was the first song that the head of our record label played us and it was the standout choice for our debut single. We all felt it was really catchy and just a great pop record. There were a few tracks for us to consider, but from that very early selection nothing matched up to 'Carry You'. And the words were really something that everyone would know us for. It stayed true to who we were as a band.

JAYMI: Exactly. With 'Carry You', something just struck us; the lyrics were so relevant to our journey on *The X Factor*, the words spoke about what our fans go through day in, day out. We speak to our fans a lot and they are all there for each other; they are there for us too and we very much believe in supporting them, so the lyrics felt very relevant to us. It was important that we had a single that meant something to us, so that we believed in what we were singing, and of course so that we enjoyed singing it. 'Carry You' was just the song that we kept going back to, the one that we kept singing all the time.

JOSH: TOTALLY. THE LYRICS DO MEAN SO MUCH TO US; THEY RELATE TO OUR STORY. IT'S A GOOD REFLECTION OF HOW THE FANS HELPED US: THEY DIRECTLY HELPED UNION J FORM, THEN THEY HELPED US THROUGH EACH WEEK IN **X FACTOR.** THE FANS WERE THERE ALL OF THE WAY FOR US, SO IT DOES RELATE TO THEM AND HOW WE HAVE GOT TO KNOW THEM.

JJ: It's always going to be difficult to know which song to release first . . . but that was the one. We actually cut about six or seven songs before we decided . . .

JOSH: We just had a good feeling about that song. It was like we were saying, 'Our group has arrived, we are out of *X Factor*, this is us . . . as Union J!' I will be totally honest and say the first couple of times I heard it I wasn't sure, but then it really started to grow on me and all of a sudden we recorded it and then . . . wow! I realised it is just the most amazing pop song.

GEORGE: Steve Mac wrote the single; he has worked with some of the biggest names in pop music. He was really good to work with. It was really fun to be able to get into the studio and have fun messing around with songs. Steve's studio is like a spaceship. It's like walking into the starship *Enterprise* or something! Flashing lights everywhere – it's really cool! He's a great guy. We spent so much time in the studio that you kind of get to know those people you are working with, and he's kind of become like an uncle to us. Really cool.

JOSH: I always wanted to work with Steve when I was in all my other bands so to actually be in his studio was amazing. I'm used to recording in a shed so to be in a top studio in London with such a famous producer was amazing. It suddenly felt very real.

We were a bit shy at first, but we got through a few songs and formed a bond where we could kind of tell him what we thought and have more of a productive relationship. So, yes, we were a bit scared at the beginning but we quickly felt at home!

JAYMI: I remember the studio work being just so easy and fun. We went in each day and it was so much fun. The most exciting time; what a privilege. We recorded the single in about a week but then we kept going back and tweaking – it seemed like for months! – just trying to perfect the song. Little things like a word here or a different note there . . . We just wanted it to be perfect.

JJ: Around this time we all moved to north London to live in the same apartment complex. I'm a bit of a country boy at heart, as you know, so that was a bit of a change! But we're not too far from the countryside if I ever need some clean, fresh air! But I can't deny it's handy living where we are because we can live and breathe the band 24/7.

JJ: THE MOMENT WE FIRST HEARD OUR SINGLE ON THE RADIO WAS PRETTY EMOTIONAL.

WE WERE IN A RADIO STATION TO DEBUT THE SONG LIVE ON AIR. NOW, OBVIOUSLY WE WERE REALLY HAPPY WITH THE TUNE AND WE WERE ALSO VERY FAMILIAR WITH IT, HAVING HEARD IT FOR MONTHS, BUT EVEN SO I WAS REALLY NERVOUS BEFOREHAND BECAUSE YOU DON'T KNOW WHAT RESPONSE YOU WILL GET. WE PLAYED THE SONG AND THE RESPONSE WAS AMAZING — EVERYONE REALLY LIKED THE SONG, AND, I'VE GOT TO BE HONEST, I GOT A BIT TEARY! THEN I PASSED THAT TEARFUL FEELING ON TO THE OTHER BOYS! HA HA! BUT IT WAS A REALLY NICE MOMENT FOR US ALL.

GEORGE: You did, JJ! But, hey, we didn't have much time to relax, did we? In the weeks leading up to the single's release we literally worked non-stop. It was mad: radio tours, TV appearances like *Loose Women* and *Britain's Got More Talent*, loads of photo shoots, magazines – really hardcore!

JAYMI: This was our chance – we had all worked so hard for this opportunity and now we had the moment to put the single out and make our mark.

JOSH: We went everywhere, every day was twenty-two hours – just two hours sleep each night – but do you know what? We loved every second of it! It was manic but great fun at the same time. We worked so hard but it was all worth it in the end.

JJ: Waiting to hear the chart position was nerve-wracking, though! That Sunday was really anxious . . . but we needn't have worried . . .

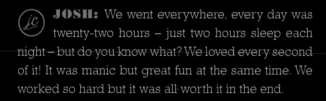

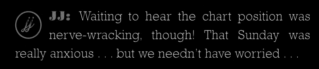

JAYMI: Absolutely! Because we charted at number six! And even more amazing was the fact that it was officially the most competitive and bestselling Top Ten for singles for five years! So we were in there mixing with the likes of Robin Thicke, Naughty Boy, Olly Murs, Jessi J, Daft Punk . . . Some of these were the biggest singles for years and so to be up there with them was a dream come true.

JOSH: We had had a tough, competitive year in *X Factor* and now the charts were tough too. But we managed to get in there and we were all delighted! It was just crazy to think that we had got a single in the charts!

JJ: IT MEANS SO MUCH.
TO KNOW THAT WE HAD THE CHANCE TO RELEASE THAT SINGLE WAS REALLY HUMBLING, AND TO THINK THAT PEOPLE BELIEVE IN US AND SUPPORT US, WE ARE REALLY GRATEFUL FOR THAT.

GEORGE: Like Jaymi says, to be in the top ten among those big songs was a privilege. We sold nearly 100,000 records in the first two weeks, so that was unreal. It just shows that hard work pays off; we all feel it is similar to the start we made in *X Factor*. We are now really motivated to knuckle down and work non-stop for the debut album and tour. We want to get every little aspect of Union J absolutely right.

JOSH: Completely agree with you, George, hundred per cent. We are so happy with the success of 'Carry You' but obviously in the future we would like to progress and get a top five, then maybe a top three and – who knows? – one day a number one. We are so ready to work incredibly hard and aim to just get better and better.

JJ: We've got our debut tour coming up and that will be incredible. Obviously we loved the *X Factor* tour but this time it will be our first chance to have our own production, our own team, our own fans. Just knowing that everyone in each venue will be there to see us is an amazing prospect. We can't wait to hear you all singing along to our songs! We've been told that to book a tour as big as ours will be after just one single is unprecedented in music, and what's even more incredible is that the demand for tickets in the first few days was so great that the shows will be a total sell-out!

JAYMI: That's a dream situation, isn't it, JJ? What's particularly special about the tour is that it perfectly reflects the closeness of the relationship we have with our fans, completely. This is everyone's chance to meet up with us and have the most amazing night. moving forward with Union J. What is clear from the success of 'Carry You' is that our first single has given us room to progress as a band. We have laid down a marker, do you know what I mean? It has started the album off very well; the debut album will be the best it can be, and we are really looking forward to all our fans hearing the record!

These past few crazy months have been a great start to our time in the industry; time to progress, and we are working with all these amazing songwriters and producers, so we are very excited about what is coming next for us.

THE THREE OTHER GUYS IN UNION J ARE MY BROTHERS.

WE HAVE BEEN THROUGH SO MUCH TOGETHER. THERE HAVE BEEN SO MANY PIVOTAL MOMENTS WHEN WE BONDED AND WHEN WE CAME TOGETHER AS A TEAM: PREPARING FOR AND THEN HEARING THE RESULT OF JUDGES' HOUSES, THE AWFUL FIRST WEEK OF THE SHOW REALLY TESTED US, ALL THOSE TIMES WE WERE IN THE BOTTOM TWO, THE HOURS AND HOURS OF REHEARSALS, AND ALL THE HARD WORK WE PUT INTO MAKING UNION J THE VERY BEST WE COULD MAKE IT . . . WE FEEL LIKE WE HAVE NEVER BEEN TIGHTER AND CLOSER AND IT'S EXCITING TO THINK THAT WE ARE ONLY JUST STARTING, YET WE HAVE THAT BOND, THAT CHEMISTRY, THAT CLOSENESS.

JJ: I would say to anyone who is thinking of doing *X Factor* it is the most amazing experience! We were going to premieres, Disneyland, performing to ten million people every week, being given expert advice and chatting to the judges . . . The lessons you learn and the things you experience are just mind-blowing. You experience massive mixed emotions on that show, but it is the best thing to do, *EVER*, if you are into your music.

As for the future, we just can't wait to get our music out there, to hear and see the fans' reactions, to go on tour and hopefully to play to as many of you as possible. It has been an amazing journey so far and, of course, it is only just beginning . . .

JAYMI: We are so excited about the future. We've got a record deal, brilliant management behind us and an amazing life ahead of us. It doesn't matter where we came on *X Factor*, it's what we do now. After all those years of trying and failing, after all those rejections and let-downs – for all of us – I just kept thinking, *This time it is really happening!* It is amazing how it's turned out and I couldn't have asked for a better situation to be in. I think there is no limit to where Union J can go if we work hard and be the best we can be.

If you can learn anything from our story so far it is to never give up. Don't get complacent; fight, work hard and it will pay off. If you ever think about doing anything with your life, commit to it one hundred per cent regardless of whether you are skint, have nowhere to live, if people say you are going to fail . . . If you believe in yourself then work hard with what you have been given and it will pay off. You can't expect things to come and land in your lap, you will need help, but when you get that break it's about what you do with that opportunity, and what you choose to do with your life that makes the difference. And Union J is going to do everything in our power to make sure this is the most exciting time of our lives!

'**JAYMI:** IF YOU CAN LEARN ANYTHING FROM OUR STORY SO FAR IT IS TO NEVER GIVE UP. DON'T GET COMPLACENT; FIGHT, WORK HARD AND IT WILL PAY OFF. IF YOU EVER THINK ABOUT DOING ANYTHING WITH YOUR LIFE, COMMIT TO IT ONE HUNDRED PER CENT REGARDLESS OF WHETHER YOU ARE SKINT, HAVE NOWHERE TO LIVE, IF PEOPLE SAY YOU ARE GOING TO FAIL . . . IF YOU BELIEVE IN YOURSELF THEN WORK HARD WITH WHAT YOU HAVE BEEN GIVEN AND IT WILL PAY OFF.'

THANKS

JAYMI: First I want to say thanks to God for blessing me and making my dreams come true! To our amazing J Cats – none of this would have been possible if it hadn't been for the incredible support you have given us every step of the way, and especially for all the love you gave me when I decided to come out with who I am. Be true to yourself and rock it and never let anyone make you feel anything other than fabulous! Next to my family: thank you to Mum, my rock, who has given me the most incredible upbringing and always put my dreams before her own; to Dad, who has given me nothing but love and support through any choice I have made in my life; to my brother Aaron, who has always told me how proud of me he is and has become my best friend; and to my nan, Betty, who is the most phenomenal woman I have ever met, one in a million and part of the reason I am who I am today! Thank you also to every other member of my family who I love so much, including my two beautiful nephews, Callum and Oliver, and the two new Hensley arrivals due in December! I love you all so much! Next, thank you to my gay family and Barbie army! You have totally shaped me and made me the man I am today. I am so proud of my community. And to Nick and Flame, I owe you more than I could ever repay for my second start in life. I love you! Thanks to our management, Crown, our label, RCA, to Syco and Mr Simon Cowell for making the *X Factor* a reality, to Mr Louis Walsh for believing in us, and to everyone on the *X Factor* team. Thank you, Blair, for giving Triple-J a start, and Thank you to the Brit School, Sylvia Young theatre school, Theatre Space and to all my students! To the people in my life who aren't around to share this with me – my Grandad Beebop, Fluffy Nanny, Auntie Mandy and my nephew Charlie – thank you for watching over me. To my brothers George, Josh and JJ: I am so glad I get to share all of this with you! Love you. And finally, to my soulmate, Olly, who has loved me unconditionally every day and put my needs and dreams before his own – I love you for being my superstar!

JJ: My section is all about my life: the up and downs that I had to face and everyone who supported me through them. First, a massive thanks to my family and friends, who were there for me from the very start, helped me to become the man I am today and who showed me that if you believe in something and you try hard enough you will get what you want out of life. Next, a huge thank you to everyone who voted every week throughout the *X Factor* – without you, Union J would not exist. Then of course I need to thank Crown Management and Sony. They are the driving force behind Union J, making us head in the right direction and pushing us to the best of our ability. Last but not least I want to thank George, Jaymi and Josh, the three boys who have made my journey extremely special. Massive thanks to all of you!! Without your amazing support I wouldn't be living my lifelong dream. Much love,

JJx

JOSH: Where can I start? I need to begin by saying how amazing our fans are. None of this would have been possible, and I certainly wouldn't be writing a section of a book, without you! You guys are amazing and I love every single J Cat out there who has supported us on our crazy journey so far. Thank you so much to everyone who voted for us during the *X Factor*; without you guys picking up the phone we wouldn't be here today. I really do love you all and can't wait to see you all when we're on our very own tour! My biggest thank you has to go to my amazing mum. She has supported me through everything and came with me to every single audition I've ever had, which, trust me, has been loads. She urged me to go to as many as possible and always picked me up no matter how many knock-backs I got. I have so much to thank her for, and will be forever grateful. She is amazing and I love her to bits! I also have an amazing family and wouldn't swap any of them for the world. My family is my rock and I love them so very much. You all know who you are and you really do mean the world to me. I am also lucky to have a wicked group of friends back home who have supported me in everything I do. A special thank you for all the FIFA nights with my two best mates, James Mitchell and Ryan Rocastle! I would also like to thank a guy you may have heard of – Simon Cowell. If he hadn't woken up one day and decided to make the most amazing television show in the whole world then Union J wouldn't even exist! Thank you to everyone who worked on the show, to our management, Crown and to our record label, RCA. Thank you for believing in us and giving us this amazing opportunity. And arguably the most important thank you goes to my three brothers: JJ, Jaymi and George. Thank you for being in my life. I couldn't wish to be on this journey with three more amazing people. Bring it on and,

GEORGE. The only way I can start this is by thanking my four favourite girls in the whole entire world! To my amazing Nan, my crazy best friend Emily, my beautiful Auntie Mickey and most of all to Mum: I love you unconditionally. Without your support and hugs I would not be the person I am today. Thank you. Thanks to Dad and to my stepmum Row; you have always pushed me to be the best I can be and I cannot thank you enough for that. Love you so much. Without my incredibly talented grandad (Dave-Busker-Harris), Uncle Jonny, Cousin Sid and Uncle Tim, music would have never been such a huge part of my life. You have all inspired me to follow my dream. Thank you. I also cannot thank all my brothers and sisters enough. Tom, Will, Harriet, Leo, Archie, Annabelle, Louisa, Spencer and Carmon, you have all been there through thick and thin and brought me so much happiness. Love you all to the moon and back! For the countless fun sleepovers and adventures I want to thank Lisa, Brad, Bron and Amelia ('GAMESCUBEN!') and thank you also to all of my true friends who have been there for me from the beginning. You know who you are! Thanks to Crown, to Mark and Debbie (Mumma) Hargreaves – I'm so happy to have you all in my life and to be part of a new extended family! – and to Sony and RCA. Endless thanks to everyone on the team for believing in us. Special thanks to Martin Roach, who helped us tell our story, Elise Dumontet for her brilliant photography, Daniel Bunyard for his boundless enthusiasm, Sarah Fraser for designing our book, John Hamilton, Alison O'Toole, Nick Lowndes, Tim Broughton, Katya Shipster, Tom Weldon, Louise Moore and the rest of the team at Penguin. We won't let you down! J Cats – without your support our dreams would never have become reality. Thanks to you, we don't have to close our eyes to see our dreams. If I could give you all monkey hugs, I would! <3 Love you! Finally, Jaymi, Josh and JJ: my three brothers and best friends. Love you,

George